Conquering the Crowded Curriculum

KATHLEEN GOULD LUNDY

Pembroke Publishers Limited

© 2015 Pembroke Publishers
538 Hood Road
Markham, Ontario, Canada L3R 3K9
www.pembrokepublishers.com

Distributed in the U.S. by Stenhouse Publishers
480 Congress Street
Portland, ME 04101
www.stenhouse.com

All rights reserved.
No part of this publication may be reproduced in any form or by any means electronic or mechanical, including photocopy, scanning, recording, or any information, storage or retrieval system, without permission in writing from the publisher. Excerpts from this publication may be reproduced under licence from Access Copyright, or with the express written permission of Pembroke Publishers Limited, or as permitted by law.

Every effort has been made to contact copyright holders for permission to reproduce borrowed material. The publishers apologize for any such omissions and will be pleased to rectify them in subsequent reprints of the book.

Library and Archives Canada Cataloguing in Publication

Lundy, Kathleen Gould, author
    Conquering the crowded curriculum / Kathleen Gould Lundy.

Includes bibliographical references and index.
Issued in print and electronic formats.
ISBN 978-1-55138-294-4 (pbk.).--ISBN 978-1-55138-860-1 (pdf)

1. Teachers--Time management. 2. Lesson planning. 3. Classroom management.
I. Title.

LB2838.8.L86 2014   371.102'4   C2013-907488-0
                                              C2013-907489-9

Editor: Kate Revington
Cover Design: John Zehethofer
Typesetting: Jay Tee Graphics Ltd.

Printed and bound in Canada
9 8 7 6 5 4 3 2 1

Contents

Preface with Acknowledgments   5

Introduction: The Curriculum Dilemma   7

   The Potential for Authentic Teaching Tapestries   7
   How to Address the Challenges   8

1: The Classroom Context — Inclusiveness   9

   Education: Putting the Destination within Everyone's Reach   9
   The Teacher Has a Strong Sense of the Students   10
   The Teacher Encourages Students' Positive Sense of Self   11
   The Teacher Has an Evolving Sense of Self   13
   The Teacher Has a Sense of "Place"   14
   Inclusion Activities That Help Teachers Gain a Sense of Their Students   17
   Inclusion Exercises That Promote Students' Positive Sense of Self   19
   Inclusion Practices That Foster Teachers' Evolving Sense of Self   24
   Approaches to Fostering Teachers' Sense of Community   27
   Assuming Responsibility for the World   29

2: Stop, Look, and Listen — Identity   30

   The Equity Agenda as Journey   30
   Stop to Take Stock   31
   Look in Multiple Ways   34
   Listen to Voices Silent and Heard   35
   Becoming Part of a Movement   37
   Games That Promote Identity   37
   From I to We   40
   And Everyone's Voice Was Strong   45
   The Potential for a New Kind of Self   47

3: Bringing the World into the Classroom — Inquiry   48

   Into New Realms of Learning   48
   A Process Driven by Four Purposes   49
   Towards Collaborative Inquiry   54
   Kinds of Questions for an Inquiry-Based Classroom   55
   Developing Rich Questions: Six Approaches   57
   How to Support Students in Fulfilling Their Research Tasks   65
   Ways to Share Initial Findings and Present New Understandings   67
   Line Masters   69

4: How to Make a Crowded Curriculum Work — Integration *71*

    Planning with Integration in Mind *72*
    Exploring the Potential of Themes *74*
    Images of Snow: Integrating by Theme within a Subject *76*
    Leaving Home: Integrating by Theme and across Subjects *81*
    Disappearance: Integrating by Theme, within Subjects, and across Subjects *88*
    Models of Innovative and Integrated Inquiry Projects *96*
    Culminating Events for Integrated Units *99*
    A Team Approach to Curriculum Integration *103*
    Line Masters *104*

5: With New and Open Eyes — Innovation *107*

    Striving towards Moments of Significance *107*
    Characteristics of Effective Teaching *108*
    Images of Dynamic Teaching: The 6 Rs *113*
    Effects of Innovative Practice on Teachers *117*
    Thirty Arts Strategies to Move Learning Forward *119*
    Never Looking Back *136*

    Bibliography *139*
    Index *141*

Preface with Acknowledgments

This book has been a long time in the making. It was delayed for a number of reasons — in particular, the death of my husband, Chuck, my best friend, who was a brilliant teacher and lifelong advocate for the kind of teaching that I describe in the five chapters of this book. Chuck, a professor at the Faculty of Education at the University of Toronto, had a brilliant mind and insisted that his students do work of significance, always with a degree of artistry and with thoughtful purpose. He influenced me in so many ways and was a sounding board throughout the years. He listened to my teaching stories and always offered profound responses, not judging my mistakes harshly but helping me think how I might have approached things differently. He constantly encouraged me to invent and reinvent my teaching practices. When he died, I felt I had lost not only my support but also my inspiration.

Although writing was something that I had often relied on to get me through difficult times, after Chuck died, I found it impossible to write (or read). It was more than writer's block. I felt that my "writing mind" was inaccessible and, try as I might, I could not find the key. For me, everything came to a standstill because of shock, fear, feelings of inadequacy, isolation, depression, and loneliness. The cycle seemed to be never-ending, and procrastination became my next-door neighbor, hovering close by all the time.

Now things have shifted. In June of 2014, I was awarded a Ministry of Education research grant to investigate innovative, integrative, and imaginative teaching practices in 10 Ontario school boards. Initially, I did not think that I could possibly fulfill the project. I spent the summer in a worried state. But, after the contract was signed with the Council of Ontario Directors of Education in September, I began to believe in myself again. I *had* to write. I *had* to research. I *had* to imagine new ideas again. The project is called *All I's on Education: Imagination, Integration, Innovation*. It is designed to encourage teachers and students to select and work artistically with common concepts, contexts, ideas, themes, issues, and relationships found in various disciplines.

As I began to design the project with my research colleagues, my belief in myself started to return, and I became excited about encouraging teachers and administrators who work in complex, diverse school systems to think about innovative ways to deliver integrated curriculum at both the elementary and secondary levels. I realized that I knew this stuff — that I had advocated for this kind of teaching and learning throughout my career — and now I had the ministry's permission and support to do the work and report back on what I was discovering about the experience. The bonus was that I was able to write again.

I want to thank my publisher, Mary Macchiusi, for her kindness, patience, and understanding during this, the most difficult time in my life. Mary never gave up on me. She visited me at my farmhouse right after Chuck died, bought me chocolate, gave me books to read (even though she knew I had trouble concentrating), invited me out for lunch, took me to the Victoria Day parade in Victoria, British Columbia, welcomed me into her house for dinner, kept in touch, and just believed that I would break out of this locked space and write again.

And I have.

So, here is the book. I thank my editor, Kate Revington, who was so patient, kind, diplomatic, and encouraging throughout this whole process. I owe her a great debt and can only hope that my next book (if there is one) will have an easier passage into the light. I hope that teachers will find the ideas in this book useful and that the concepts presented here will trigger their imaginations to produce innovative ways of teaching so that they can conquer the crowded curriculum that awaits them.

Introduction: The Curriculum Dilemma

Longing to Teach in Ways That Make Sense

"If you want to build a ship, don't drum up people to collect wood and don't assign them tasks and work, but rather teach them to long for the endless immensity of the sea."
— Antoine de Saint-Exupéry

Over the last decade, I have worked with elementary and secondary school teachers and school leaders as they come to terms with what is being asked of them by 21st century educational standards, theories, curriculum, and procedures. The pressures to *adapt* and *adopt* have been overwhelming for many of them: educators have been asked to be more accountable, more imaginative, more inclusive, and more flexible all at the same time. Teachers are now expected to *adopt* an inquiry-based, project-based approach in their teaching and to *adapt* various methodologies to include online and technological advances. They are being asked to *adapt* to new ways of assessing learning and are required to *adopt* culturally relevant approaches to meet the needs of increasingly diverse student populations. As I watch them work feverishly hard in an effort to "do it all," my heart has gone out to them.

The work over the past 10 years has been pleasurable, but also intense with underlying feelings of inadequacy and worry. Teachers often ask me: "How can I do it all? I really want to teach this way, but I worry that students won't be able to pass the tests that are coming their way. Should I teach this way for a little bit and then revert to the kind of teaching that is going to get the scores that our school badly needs?" I have felt the tensions that teachers experience in their practice. They want to do what is required by their districts, but they also long to have some autonomy as well as agency: to act on their own sense of what is right, good, and true for their students and for themselves in the various contexts in which they teach.

As I work with teachers of varying levels of experience, I am always moved by the efforts of all of them to gain new knowledge and skills, find resources that their students will connect to, and raise the experience of teaching to new heights. Crucial to the success of this work are a number of factors: a commitment to this new kind of collaborative, inquiry-based teaching; support of the classroom as a negotiated place, where students' questions lead the discussion and inquiry; the permission (and encouragement) of the school administration for this kind of teaching to take place; adjustments in the school schedule/calendar; and the investment in the enterprise by teachers, students, parents, and the school community.

The Potential for Authentic Teaching Tapestries

I hope that the ideas represented here help teachers think about what is possible if we approach teaching from a collaborative, imaginative stance where learning among subjects and in relation to the real world is connected. I hope teachers will see that the links are not forced, but that the common narratives are blended together in ways that make sense. I encourage teachers to work collaboratively and creatively — to tease out common ideas, themes, and approaches that are present in the curriculum — and then weave authentic teaching tapestries, where content knowledge and understanding are drawn from one subject discipline and used to enrich and apply to others.

This book will help teachers work together to create and teach curriculum that is imaginative, integrated, inquiry based, and innovative. Precise and proven ways of teaching and assessing are introduced, and teachers are encouraged to look at the curriculum expectations of the subjects they are responsible for and then work with each other to develop inquiry projects that meet the needs and interests of their students. I provide ways for teachers to sift out what is important from the mass of material in front of them so that they can seamlessly "connect the curriculum dots."

How to Address the Challenges

This book is intended to be a practical resource that explores innovative ways for teachers to "conquer" the many curricular challenges they face in diverse, contemporary classrooms. It describes worthwhile projects that they can co-create with their colleagues and students so that learning about something of significance is done in innovative ways from a variety of perspectives.

Here, I describe ways that elementary and secondary school teachers can set up integrated webs of contextualized learning so that students are engaged in curricular material that matters to them.

- In Chapter 1, I outline what it means to teach in inclusive ways.
- In Chapter 2, I encourage all of us to stop, look, and listen to our students so that we can plan and implement culturally responsive and relevant pedagogy.
- In Chapter 3, I explore how teachers can learn to take risks in their teaching so that their students see different perspectives, think critically and imaginatively about ideas, work with others to explore material in various contexts, and represent new knowledge in precise, artistic, and profound ways.
- In Chapter 4, I present and use as models several comprehensive planned projects that carefully and skillfully integrate curriculum areas.
- In Chapter 5, I call out for this kind of work to be supported by educators who want to work in new ways, take risks in their teaching, and challenge their colleagues to come on the journey with them. Advocacy for innovative thinking is reinforced by a range of effective ways to teach.

I hope that *Conquering the Crowded Curriculum* will inspire teachers to teach in new ways and never look back.

1 The Classroom Context — Inclusiveness

Teaching towards the Ideal
"Teaching as an ethical enterprise goes beyond presenting what already is; it is teaching towards what ought to be."
— William Ayers, *To Teach: The Journey of a Teacher*, page 141

Many years ago, I came across a powerful image on the front of *The New Yorker* magazine. I bought the magazine, cut out the image, and used it for a long time, projecting it on overhead projectors in gymnasia, conference workshop areas, classrooms, and staff rooms.

I have since lost the picture, but I remember it clearly. The drawing was of a beautiful, magical subway car in which "Silence, Please" was displayed in a few prominent places. People of all ages were sitting around a large, rectangular, wooden table, reading various things — newspapers, comics, and books. (I am sure that if the artist were drawing a similar piece today, many at the table would be reading their phones or tablets.) A few people were holding books, but you could tell that they had stopped for a moment to think. Down the center of the table were a number of those wonderful brass reading lamps with the green shades that lend such a lovely, intimate glow. There were also signs on the billboards above people's heads, including one about writer's block, if I remember correctly. The sign encouraged people to keep going.

Education: Putting the Destination within Everyone's Reach

I loved this subway car image and introduced it in workshops with teachers because it made me think of schools and learning. As I projected the image, I would say to my audience: "If only schools and classrooms could be like this. Everyone would be warm and have a seat. Everyone would be assured of their destination. Everyone would be given equal opportunities. The choices displayed in the advertisements and billboards would represent constant reminders of the future that awaits. The environment would be aesthetically pleasing as well as utilitarian. People would be given an array of genres and ways to learn and read. There would be time to think. There would be a coziness, a collectivity, and a beauty that would encourage us to be together to learn."

I would point out as well that, although the conductor was missing from the image, the subway train was clearly conceived by someone who knew what he or she was doing. When the analogy is extended to the classroom again, we can say that teachers conceptualize an inclusive classroom. They work hard to make sure that everyone is welcome and honored for who they are and where they are from. They help children on their education journey. They also give students hope for the future. They ensure that the destination is within reach for everyone.

Inclusive classrooms are places where students feel they belong, where they are safe to express themselves, accepted for who they are and where they are from, and challenged to learn in new ways about themselves, others, and the complex world in which they live. Students enter these rooms knowing that people (both

You may find it interesting to read *Engaging Paulo Freire's Pedagogy of Possibility: From Blind to Transformative Optimism,* by César Augosto Rossatto (published by Rowman & Littlefield in 2004).

their teachers and their peers) will support, accept, and encourage them. Inclusive classrooms have a constant, silent beat of acceptance to them.

As Paulo Freire writes, inclusive classrooms provide a "pedagogy of possibility" to all who are in them. So, what does it mean to teach inclusively, or provide a pedagogy of possibility? In my opinion, four conditions need to be in place:

1. The teacher has a strong sense of the students.
2. The teacher encourages students' positive sense of self.
3. The teacher has an evolving sense of self.
4. The teacher has a sense of place — he or she knows the families and the local communities, and understands the cultural and environmental geography that surrounds the school.

These four frames — a teacher's sense of student, a student's sense of self, a teacher's sense of self, and a teacher's sense of the "place" in which he or she teaches — are key to effective and inclusive teaching. They allow for the emergence of a culture of critical consciousness and care.

They are elaborated in the next four sections.

The Teacher Has a Strong Sense of the Students

First of all, teachers in inclusive classrooms have a sense of their students. They find out, by various means, who is in the room and plan accordingly. "Location, location, location" is not only a real-estate mantra. From the first encounter, teachers take stock of students' locations, or who they are in terms of race, ethnicity, gender, sexual orientation, socio-economic class, and more. They acknowledge where they are from, how they see themselves as learners, what their personal stories are, and so on. They rely upon this information to plan lessons that will empower everyone to find their voices and challenge them to learn. They affirm the life experiences of the students they encounter in their classrooms so that they can connect that personal information to the themes, issues, ideas, images, relationships, technologies, and languages found in the material they are studying. They know who has access to technology, who has difficulty reading and writing, and who needs more space and support to finish assignments. They know how their students learn best and who needs to be encouraged to do something out of their comfort zone. They know when to push, when to wait, when to challenge, when to comfort, when to create more complex tasks, when to lay off, when to smile, when to cajole, when to walk away, and when to come back. They know their students well.

Recognize students' unique contexts

When I was a teacher in an urban secondary school, I knew it was important to understand the locations of my students at the very beginning of the school year. From there, I could build communities of learning in which diverse voices were valued and heard.

This work was connected to what I have come to understand about "community-based education." This kind of education begins with teachers recognizing the realities of their students' locations and knowing more about their parents and families as creators of their lives, histories, and futures. I also wanted my students to become aware of the varied backgrounds and cultures of all those in the room so that we could draw on each other's strengths, knowledge, and experiences.

The Teacher Encourages Students' Positive Sense of Self

A second condition of providing a pedagogy of possibility is for teachers to encourage a positive sense of self in each of their students. This positive sense of self can support the students as they encounter difficult situations within the turmoil of their changing and challenging worlds.

Students who feel disconnected from the school experience for whatever reasons present teachers with all kinds of individual challenges. These students might have learning difficulties or find it challenging to connect with other students in the class. It takes a while to determine the best teaching approach. Often, when consulted about these kinds of students, I suggest that the best thing to do is to help students see themselves as learners — as people who have a shot at the prize — and to help them understand that the teacher is there to ensure their success.

It is important for teachers to help students gain a better sense of what they can do: to identify the gifts they bring to the classroom. Often, teachers have to re-teach students about their loveliness — to encourage, to cajole, and to make learning about their strengths and talents explicit until students find it within themselves to bloom again. Inclusive teachers are aware of how they speak to their students and consciously push against personal bias and judgment of students.

In inclusive classrooms, teachers work with teachers, parents, students, and others to co-create an environment in which all people model the qualities of respect, responsibility, and caring. Aware of their own privilege and power, they listen to what students tell them about who they are and how they learn best. Once they know that, they dig into their teaching repertoires and begin to use appropriate teaching techniques.

Part of helping students develop a positive sense of self is to choose curriculum materials that reflect back to the students, their cultural identities, and their experiences. Teachers creatively open up curriculum windows to let learning in.

Nurture student voices

Teachers in inclusive classrooms are on the lookout for who is learning and who is not. They know that the work they do with students has to matter. It has to be relevant to students' lives. Teachers cannot fake being interested. They have to really care about what makes their students tick and then find ways of connecting what they want to know with what they need to know.

Teachers listen for the silent or absent voices in their classrooms and find ways to help these students re-engage with school and with the curriculum. As they encourage them to invest personal interest and increased effort in their own learning, they nurture student voices. From my own experience, I know the benefits that teachers' sensibilities and awareness can have on students' self-esteem, academic motivation, and individual or collective successes. I know the value of addressing their emotional, physical, and intellectual needs and the importance of adults treating students with the care and respect they would extend to their own children (Grumet 1991).

"The future is worth expecting."
— Henry David Thoreau

The impact a teacher can have

Many people think that school should be a place where students get ready for life. They argue that it should be competitive, rigorous, and challenging, and should be designed to "put students through their paces" so that they emerge strong and resilient when they get out into the real world. I have no argument about the outcome, but I do think that many students are already encountering personal difficulties, sadness, and huge challenges. They are already living lives that most of us would not be able to handle. So, I say that school should not be a difficult place to be; instead, it should be a place where students are nurtured and cared for as well as challenged and taught. Teachers need to believe that every student has the potential to succeed. They also have to help students become resilient and help them believe that they can be successful.

In one of my classes at York University, I asked my students to think about what impelled them to apply to teachers college and to find a way to represent that desire to teach in a dramatic anthology which we eventually performed in front of an audience of teacher candidates and York faculty. We experimented with monologues, scenes, choral reading, the integration of tableaux, movement, and song, and many other theatre techniques. The students told stories about their practicum placements, shared anecdotes, and reflected on what they had experienced on their journey to become teachers.

One student, Danielle Miller, told a story about her host teacher and how he had a positive impact on his students. They felt empowered in his class. They felt as if they could do the work. Here is one monologue she performed at the end of the course that tells this story:

"SMART"

He said to my mentor teacher: "You know sir, I actually feel smart in this class. I've never felt smart before."
I watched him go, and I decided: I will help every kid feel smart.
Because everyone is smart. Maybe not in conventional ways, but everyone is smart.
I want to call out, shout out so they'll hear:
Don't let anybody tell you
you aren't smart
When it comes to your brain
when it comes to your heart
don't let anybody tell you
you aren't smart.
G-d gives everybody gifts and talents to use.
Don't let anyone try to confuse
you into thinking you're inadequate
because you're not smart the way other kids are.
Find you're smart, it's there, I know
even if it's unknown now.
Nobody's perfect everywhere
but we've all got some flair, somewhere.
And I will seek out yours and celebrate it
celebrate you, not a level 3 or 2.
If school prepares you for life
then learn this now:

> Take a vow
> to be the best you can be
> because here's the reality.
> You've got something special that only you can do.
> It belongs to you.
> Never let anybody tell you
> you aren't smart
> when it comes to your work, when it comes to your art.
> Sure, you've got strengths and weaknesses, next steps, places to go
> but here's one thing you must always know:
> You are smart.

The Teacher Has an Evolving Sense of Self

A third condition involved with teachers promoting a pedagogy of possibility is for the teacher to have an evolving personal sense of self. Indeed, as Greenberg (1969, 20–21) records, the teacher's humanity is vital to the ability of students to learn:

> Within the teacher's emotional life are the forces that most powerfully affect the entire teaching process. The human, emotional qualities of the teacher are the very heart of teaching. No matter how much emphasis is placed on such other qualities in teaching as educational technique, technology, equipment or buildings, the humanity of the teacher is the vital ingredient if children are to learn.

Teachers' personal sense of self bears on their effectiveness in the classroom. Teachers of inclusive classrooms know their strengths and are honest about what they need to learn to teach even more effectively. They take risks in their teaching, are sensitive to cultural factors, and are open to new ideas and varying interpretations. They are also aware of their own biases and strive to look for students' strengths rather than deficits.

Research tells us that teachers' perceptions — what some call their "their cultural lens" — determine, in part, the level of engagement and academic achievement of their students. Children respond to the generosity of their teachers' perceptions of them and the interest their teachers convey about them.

So, how do teachers adjust perceptions and develop a greater awareness of how their sense of self affects the classroom dynamic? Teachers are required to take note of personal biases and how their first impressions of students might have to be adjusted once they realize that the students are being shaped by conditions very different from the ones that shaped them. Teachers need to work at being aware of who is in the room. They also need to continue to take courses and challenge themselves to think critically of what they are teaching and how they are teaching it. It helps if they have a certain confidence and a desire to learn from mistakes.

The journey to imaginative teaching and joyful learning is full of interruptions, tentative discoveries, negative attitudes, lack of resources, and questioning by some colleagues. I believe, however, that the work is worth all the disappointments, self-doubt, and worry. Initially, our rewards will be small — the glimmer of understanding, the thankful parent's phone call — but these will be followed by the students' excitement about their projects and finally, their triumphs in understanding and comprehension. They will find themselves part of the club

---

A Challenge: Valuing Everyone

"At home I was valued. At school it was different. How do we give everyone value in the circle? We all come together to learn. How do we hold each other up?"
— Lee Maracle, at the Ontario Federation of Teachers/Ontario Association of Deans of Education conference, York University, February 2014

of people who think, speak, and write with an understanding of audience, of the power of metaphor, of the subtlety of nuance, and of the importance of voice.

As William Ayers wrote so beautifully in a 2004 article in *Rethinking Schools*:

> Humanistic teachers need to develop an entirely different rhythm, sometimes in the cracks and crevices of the classrooms we are given. We begin with a many-eyed approach: an eye on your students and an eye on yourself, an eye on the environment for learning and an eye on the contexts within which your work is embedded. You need an eye on reality and another on possibility.
>
> You might end each day asking, "What didn't I do well today? Could I have done better with this student or that one? What alternatives exist?" And you might start the next day forgiving yourself for your lapses and shortcomings, ready to start again. Without self-criticism, teachers can become too easily satisfied, and then self-righteous. But without acceptance they are vulnerable to self-loathing, to berating themselves unnecessarily. Criticism and forgiveness — this is the path to wisdom in teaching. We are, each one of us, a work-in-progress. We are pilgrims who see our students as unruly sparks of meaning-making energy on a voyage through their lives. We, too, are on a journey. Let's create a teaching life worthy of our teaching values.

The Teacher Has a Sense of "Place"

See "Images of Dynamic Teaching: The 6 Rs," in Chapter 5.

Teachers have a sense of place and are aware of the communities that lie beyond the classroom: families, artists, businesses, police, fire department, emergency services, cultural institutions . . . these are all communities. Teachers know, value, respect, and take into account the people in the communities in which they teach.

In particular, teachers consider the challenges faced by some of their students' families. These problems may be connected to mental health, poverty, divorce, illness, the death of a grandparent, and more. The teachers do not judge, but they allow what they know to inform their teaching practices and help them think about and implement differentiated instruction and community involvement.

Become aware of structural inequities

Relationships at the Center
In my research in the 10 schools that are part of the *All I's on Education* project, I discovered that the work of innovation is very much connected to relationships: not only relationships between teachers and students but relationships among students and with their parents, families, and the communities in which they live. There also is a sense of school as a place of possibility where relationships to people and to learning are enhanced every day. As students are encouraged to work together on relevant curriculum, they develop an awareness of other perspectives. They learn to listen to and respect diverse viewpoints. They develop a relationship to learning that takes into account other ideas they had not thought of before.

Over three years, I taught a School and Society course at the Ontario Institute for Studies in Education. The course focuses on the relationships between education, language, pedagogy, and social justice. Teacher candidates are encouraged to challenge the taken-for-granted, normalized, and often routine practices connected to structural inequities in schools and the communities of which they are a part. In addressing the inequities that face schools, classrooms, and communities, the course calls upon teacher candidates to explore anti-oppression theories and their own roles and responsibilities to promote social justice.

I found ways to teach equity and social justice through drama by linking cross-curricular approaches to education that challenge racism, sexism, ethnocentrism, homophobia, classism, and discrimination against persons with disabilities. I resisted just lecturing or having students respond only through discussion of the readings. Although I did some of that, I endeavored to give my students a taste of drama. Planning to have them experience it was something of a risk: the number of students in the class made the work challenging.

Somehow, I managed to structure the work so that the students were attentive, engaged, and challenged to work in role. In one session I worked with the following questions:

- How can we tap into our own biases and see life from other perspectives?
- What is the impact of poverty, hunger, and disenfranchisement on education? How can we use drama to understand these issues?
- How can this awareness help you serve your students and your school community in better ways?

We worked with a short story called "The Party" by Nigel Gray. The story is about a child from a poor family who often goes hungry. The child is asked to a birthday party but is told he cannot go. He disobeys his mother (who is at work), escapes from his locked flat by jumping out a window, and walks up and down the street in the rain until brought into the party by the birthday girl's mother.

After I read the short story to the class, we did some tableaux work; then, the students got into small groups, where one member volunteered to play the protagonist's mother. The rest of the group representing a school team of social workers, classroom teachers, psychologists, administrators, and so on interviewed the mother. The interview revealed a lot about the mother's life, such as the pressures she was under to provide for her son, working three jobs without sufficient funds for childcare. The School and Society students found that they were able to adopt a role, sustain it, speak as someone else, imagine the mother's predicament, and gain a different perspective. Most of the 76 students were engaged on a deep level in the role playing.

The drama ended with an Inner/Outer Circle of students reading their writing in role as the mother, the school principal, the teacher, the psychologist, or the social worker (see page 127 for more on the Inner/Outer Circle strategy).

Learn to respond with empathy

After the drama, I handed out the following letter:

> Dear Parents:
> Our class is going on a field trip to the Toronto Symphony on Friday, December 6. This is a fabulous opportunity for your child to hear the best music that that the world has to offer. The cost of the field trip is $15.00. Please sign the permission slip and attach the money (a cheque is best) made out to the school. <u>I need this money by next Friday at the latest</u>.
>
> Our plan is to take the TTC. We will leave the school at 12:15. Please pack a litter-less lunch and snack. We will return to the school in time for dismissal. I will be able to take 3 parent volunteers to the symphony. Please let me know by email if you would like to attend. <u>First come, first served</u>.
>
> As well, our Poetry Café will be happening at 1:30 p.m. this coming Thursday in the school gym. I am hoping that you will support your child's literacy learning by attending. Thanks to those parents who have already volunteered to bake goodies.
>
> Yours sincerely,
> Ms. Gordon
> Room 201

The letter provided a frame for us to talk about the socio-economic challenges that some families face. We discussed the letter from the lens of our imagined mother's reality. How would she feel, and what would she think when she received this letter from the school? What could she do? What can schools and school systems do to lessen the burden on families? How could the letter be rewritten so that systemic inequalities could be challenged and reduced? What other equity issues did the letter invite the teacher candidates to think about? The in-class, small-group assignment was to rewrite the letter, taking into account the mother's reality.

Here is one of the letters, which could be translated into another language, if necessary, so a parent could understand it:

> Dear Parents/Guardians:
>
> Our class is going on a field trip to the Toronto Symphony on Friday, December 6. Please sign the permission slip and put it in your child's backpack. The cost of the field trip is $15.00 and our arts funding budget is going to pay for this trip. We are planning ways to re-stock the arts budget through some fund-raising next month. Stay tuned!
>
> Our plan is to take the TTC. We will leave the school at 12:15. Please pack a lunch and a snack for your child. We will return to the school in time for dismissal. I am inviting 3 parent volunteers to come along with us to the symphony. I realize that many of you will be working or looking after other children and won't be able to come this time. Please let me know if you are interested in doing something like this, and we will try to have you come on our next field trip!
>
> As well, our Poetry Café will be happening at 1:30 p.m. this coming Thursday in the school gym. I am hoping that you will be able to come to see how much your child is learning about language and literacy. Everyone is welcome.
>
> Yours sincerely,
> Ms. Gordon
> Room 201

As a result of the experience, one student wrote the following comments:

> Today was eye-opening. I had never experienced this kind of learning before. I grew up in a country where teachers teach and students listen so being involved in this kind of drama experience was at first challenging and then quite exciting. I was amazed at the improvised responses of my peers and was moved on more than one occasion by the way that Kathy layered the voices in the drama so that we began to see the struggles that the mother encountered every single day. When we had a chance to hear the mother speak, a different kind of feeling took over the room. The mother was strong and very brave. She loved her son and wanted the best for him. She was so stretched financially. It was a very emotional experience — and I was so involved.

Another student reflected on the class in this way:

> The letter that Kathy handed out was very problematic on so many levels. The people in my group all agreed that we would not have responded with the knowledge, awareness, critical insight, and empathy that we did without having done the drama before we got the letter. We understood the context because we had met the people who are most affected by the inequality of school systems. I am not sure that I have the confidence to try this kind of teaching yet, but I certainly want to learn more about how to engage students through drama.

Inclusion Activities That Help Teachers Gain a Sense of Their Students

What follows are activities that foster a non-competitive culture of listening and co-operation and an ethic of hearing and valuing everyone's voice. The purpose of these activities is to help students get to know one another, learn to respect themselves and others, value differing opinions, share common experiences, and work towards a critical understanding of complex relationships and ideas.

Playing co-operative games is a wonderful way to begin to know your students and build a sense of inclusion and community in the classroom. Games have a way of distracting students from feelings of inadequacy. In fact, the rules of games are often liberating because they make each of us feel safe to participate. Rules can be negotiated and created by the group if necessary. The important thing is that the rules are freely accepted by all — so that fun can happen within a tight structure.

Atom

Ask students to push the desks aside and make a circle in the space.

Have students "walk to the empty spaces in the room" without bumping into one another. Have them walk quickly, change direction, walk on tiptoes, walk backwards, walk sideways, and so on. On a signal such as a tambourine tap or a drumbeat, have them freeze. Congratulate them and then tell them to relax.

Advise them that they are going to repeat the activity, but this time you will be calling out directions such as "Atom 3!" or "Atom 5!" When you say, "Atom 3!" they will behave as if they are atoms and join up with the students who are closest to them to form a group of three. They are to quickly learn each other's names. They are then to walk throughout the room again as a group of three. If you say, "Atom 5!" they are to form a group of five. If anyone is left over, students are to hide those people in the group constellation. Students continue to learn one another's names.

Circulate around the classroom and check to find the extra people hidden in the groups. Keep the groups moving and changing until everyone has been jumbled up and can give the names of five new classmates.

Not Only *What* but *How*

When I do workshops in schools, I introduce this game to gain an opportunity to hear how students want their names pronounced. Indeed, I have them play this game every time I visit! I take special care not to mispronounce names and thus avoid embarrassing students. I never want a student to change his or her name, or anglicize it, just because I mispronounced it.

Words of Inspiration

I have never left a classroom after introducing this book without having at least one student stop me to ask if he or she could look up a birthday and a quotation. The book is a winner. It is also a way to help students hear inspirational words and understand that they have the potential to change the world in significant ways.

Simple Cues

If students feel embarrassed, tell them not to worry or overthink the action. They just need to move slightly so that the group notices them and copies their movement.

Birthday Line

Have the students arrange themselves in two equal lines, or teams. Then, have them line up in alphabetical order according to their first names. Invite them to say their names out loud so that everyone can hear each name with the correct pronunciation.

Now, on your signal, students are to arrange themselves in the order of their birthday months. They should work as quickly as possible. Prompt the students to say their birth dates out loud and ask all of the students to pay attention as they do so.

After this part of the game, ask students if they heard any birthdays to which they can make a personal connection. For example, they might say, "My sister has the same birthday as Janet," or "Rashid and I have the same birthday, and we never even knew that all last year!"

I often introduce the book *A Gift of Days: The Greatest Words to Live By* by Stephen Alcorn. Starting with January 1 and arranged by birth date, *A Gift of Days* highlights the words and ideas of 365 famous people, including Beethoven, Rosa Parks, and Maria Callas, whose words are set within their birthdays and highlight the kind of people they were and the words they lived by. For instance, American poet Emily Dickinson was born on December 10, 1830. Beside her birthday are quoted these words: "Forever is composed of nows." Often, a class will spend time looking up people's birthdays and discussing the quotations.

Back to Back/Face to Face

Have students find a partner, learn his or her name, and then stand back to back just far enough away not to be touching each other. Prompt the partners to change their position as you call out different commands, such as "Face to face," "Side to side," "Shoulder to shoulder," "Elbow to elbow," and "Elbow to shoulder." When you say, "Change partners," students find another partner, and the commands begin again. Enable students to find as many partners as possible, and encourage them to learn their names in the split second of meeting each person.

Stomp It, Name It, Clap It

This game progresses in a way that builds student confidence and challenges them to work collectively and co-operatively. I often play it with shy students who find it difficult to even look at one another. When they begin to stomp, they have to look down at their feet and watch the group communication bounce around the circle. Everyone relaxes, and some of them laugh with pleasure as I encourage the stomp to go louder, faster, in a new direction, and so on.

Stomp It: Ask the students to stand in a circle. One person begins to stomp with both feet (left and then right). The person to his or her right does the same thing, and the "stomp" is passed around the circle. Have the students pass the stomp more quickly and then with their eyes closed. Have them also pass the stomp in the opposite direction. Encourage them to go faster if they can.

Name It: First, the students say their names once as they go around the circle. The next time they each say their names, the rest of the class repeats the name out loud. The students then each say their name and do a simple action. The rest of the students say the name aloud and copy the action, and then it is the next person's turn.

Clap It: Have students remain standing in the circle, and join the circle yourself. Make eye contact with the person to your left. Clap your hands. The person on your left responds to the clap by clapping back, turns to the person on her or his left, establishes eye contact, and claps once. That person claps back and then "passes the applause" to the person on his or her left. The applause is passed around the circle until it comes back to you.

Passing the Applause

It is important for the students to maintain eye contact as they pass the applause. Students often are amazed at how the group connects, and a kind of electricity is created in the room, especially if the exercise goes quickly. You can also vary the game so that more than one clap is sent around the circle. Be sure to listen to suggestions from the students on how the exercise could be changed or adapted.

Heigh Ho!

Have students sit in chairs in a circle. Appoint someone to be "It." "It" stands in the middle of the circle and says something like, "Everyone who is wearing sandals, change places." Everyone in sandals has to move to another chair. "It" runs to a chair and sits down. The person left standing then becomes "It." "It" can then say something like, "Everyone who watched TV last night, change places!" or "Everyone who wishes it was still summer vacation, change places!" Students move or sit according to their responses. If, however, the person who plays "It" says, "Heigh ho!" then everyone must change places. Play the game quickly.

Squirrel and Tree

Students get into groups of three. Two people stand facing each other and join hands to create an arch: they are the tree. The third person crouches underneath it and becomes the squirrel. One person is designated the "caller." The caller calls out one of three things:

- *"Hunter."* If "hunter" is shouted, then all the squirrels run to a new tree. The caller then tries to steal the place of a squirrel. If successful, then the person left without a tree becomes the new caller. (The trees do not move.)
- *"Fire."* If "fire" is shouted, the trees move to a new squirrel. Each part of the tree must find a new partner to create a tree over a squirrel. The caller then tries to steal the place of a tree, leaving someone out. That person becomes the new caller.
- *"Earthquake."* If this is shouted, then everyone moves and takes a new position as either a tree or as a squirrel. Again, the caller steals someone's place, and a new caller is determined.

As students play these games, teachers notice who is comfortable, who listens well, who is shy, who is an English Language Learner, who needs to be noticed, who wants to be invisible, who needs to be taken care of, and who needs encouragement. They gain a better sense of the children in the room through active, fun ways that are not intrusive. If they participate, too, they become part of the community of people learning to work and play together.

Inclusion Exercises That Promote Students' Positive Sense of Self

Teachers can help their students gain self-awareness and a new sense of themselves and the possibilities before them by making learning as safe and welcoming as possible. As students engage in various activities, they begin to understand

Listen to the World

"Stay at your table and listen . . . Be completely quiet . . . The world will offer itself to you to be unmasked . . ."
— Franz Kafka

that there are many ways of communicating, being, responding, thinking, and representing who they are and what they are learning about themselves and others.

The first five exercises are designed to help students listen — to take in the sounds within their classroom, the sounds within their community, and the sounds that they can make with their voices, their feet, their hands, and found objects. These exercises help students go from "just listening" to becoming critical listeners. Students become more skilled at listening to the words of others and become aware of both what was said and what was not said. In general, allow students to "take time out to listen." Some might not have been granted the luxury for a long time. It is likely a good idea to start with the easier exercises.

The last two exercises in this section focus on how people uniquely see and respond to the world around them: how they read their environment.

Let's Just Listen

Ask students to close their eyes and become as comfortable as they can. Prompt them to listen to the sounds around them in the classroom. Encourage them to try to block out the noises in the hall or in the street beyond the windows. The process will likely take about 30 seconds.

Tell the students to open their eyes. Ask them the following questions:
- What sounds did you hear?
- Were there any sounds you were unaware of until we did this exercise?
- Were there any sounds you are still unsure of?
- Why do you suppose we are not aware of the sounds that surround us — perhaps the ticking of our classroom clock or the sounds of the heating fans — on a minute-by-minute basis?

Ask the students to close their eyes again. Now have them listen to all the sounds outside the classroom. Prompt them to concentrate on the sounds in the hall; then, have them listen to the sounds of the street or the playground. How many different sounds can they hear?

Do as I Say

Ask students to get into partners and decide who is *A* and who is *B*.

A is the instructor; *B* is the learner. The partners sit back to back.

B is given a piece of paper and a pencil. *A* is given a diagram.

A first describes the diagram to *B* and then provides precise instructions about what and how to draw. *A* is not allowed to see what *B* is drawing, but *B* is allowed to ask questions for clarification.

After five minutes ask the partners to face one another. *B* then shows *A* what he or she has drawn. *A* shows *B* the original diagram. They compare the two, considering these questions: What instructions were clear? How could the instructions have been clearer? What was misinterpreted? Why did this problem occur?

Have the students switch roles.

Finally, as a class, discuss these questions: How important are instructions? How important is it to listen and ask questions? What was particularly challenging about this exercise? How important was it for the person drawing to ask questions for clarification? How can this exercise be applied to real life?

"Good Morning, Your Esteemed Majesty"

This game requires precise listening skills.

Have the class sit in a circle. Ask for a volunteer to play the part of Your Esteemed Majesty. Tell the student to sit on a chair with his or her back to the audience. The Majesty is not allowed to turn around.

One member of the class volunteers to approach Your Esteemed Majesty, voice disguised, and say, "Good Morning, Your Esteemed Majesty."

If the Majesty guesses the name of the speaker correctly, the other person takes over as the Majesty, and the game continues.

Fortunately/Unfortunately

This game promotes listening and improvisation. Students have to listen carefully to one another to collaboratively build a story that makes sense.

Ask the students to sit in groups of five or six. Have them number themselves off (1-2-3-4-5). Student 1 starts a story beginning with the line "Last night, as I was coming home from work, my car broke down." Student 2 continues the story but must start her part with the word "fortunately." Student 3 continues the story but begins his sentence with "unfortunately." The words are used alternately as the story is told by each member of the group. Encourage the group members to go around the circle at least twice. Ask for volunteers to share the gist of the story with the class.

Here is how one story might go. You could use it as an example for students to understand the exercise better.

1: Last night, as I was coming home from work, my car broke down.
2: Fortunately, I had my cell phone.
3: Unfortunately, when I called home, no one answered.
4: Fortunately, I was close to a gas station.
5: Unfortunately, the gas station attendant was locking up when I arrived.
6: Fortunately, he listened to my story.
7: Unfortunately, he was rushing to the hospital because his wife was in labor.
8: Fortunately, he gave me a lift to the nearest bus station.
9: Unfortunately, I didn't have any money to buy a ticket.
10: Fortunately, the ticket agent took pity on me and lent me some money.

After they have done this activity, you may want to read them *Fortunately*, a picture book by Remi Charlip.

Two Truths and a Wish

This game promotes careful and critical listening and observation. Divide the students into pairs and ask them to decide who will be the speaker and who will be the listener. The speaker is to tell the listener three things about herself: two facts and one wish. The listener pays close attention. After the speaker has spoken, the listener guesses which statement is the wish. Once the listener has uncovered the wish, the partners change roles and repeat the exercise.

You may want to ask these questions after students do the exercise:
- Were you surprised by what you learned about your partner?
- Did any of you make the wrong assumptions about your partner's truths and wishes?
- How does this exercise encourage us to rethink our assumptions about people we do not know that well?
- How do we normally "read" people?
- From having had this discussion and sharing what we have learned about each other, what new insights did we gain about who is in the class?

Reading Identity

This exercise should be done with great sensitivity and when students are ready and safe enough to share. I most often do it with Intermediate/Senior students as a way of having them look at assumptions and how they read people.

1. Hand out an index card and a pen to each person.
2. Prompt students to choose a partner they do not know well.
3. Have the partners sit facing one another. After a few minutes, have them sit back to back.
4. Ask the following questions:
   - What do you assume is the country of origin of your partner?
   - What kinds of languages do you think your partner speaks?
   - What kinds of hobbies does this person pursue?
   - What kinds of sports does he or she engage in?
   - What interests outside school does this person have?
   - What are his or her favorite foods? favorite music?
   - Does this person own a pet? If so, what kind?
5. I then ask the students to turn to one another and talk about what they have written on the card. They talk about what they assume to be true and find out whether they are right. Their partner responds to the assumptions and clarifies who he or she is.
6. This powerful exercise is dependent on a certain degree of trust in the room. It can be unpacked by having the whole class address the following questions:
   - Did we "read" our partners right?
   - What did we get right? What did we get wrong?
   - What assumptions did we make that were right? What made us have these assumptions?
   - What assumptions did we make that were wrong? Why do we have these wrong assumptions?
   - How did this exercise make you feel? When your partner read you wrong, what was your response?
   - How important is it for us to tell the stories of our identities in the midst of being misunderstood?
   - Why do we have these misperceptions of each other?
   - How do we unlearn these things?
   - How do we encourage each other to listen to our stories of identity and culture?
   - How do we help others to check their assumptions? Why is it important to do so?

No One Sees...

When I teach, I often introduce images where there is a certain degree of human drama — an event that requires us to think and feel about something outside of our experience. An avid Twitter fan, I find images on Twitter from History in Pictures that spark amazing conversations among students in all grades.

A wonderful book I recommend using to promote a sense of inclusion in the classroom is *No One Saw* by Bob Raczka. Its message is that no one sees the world in quite the same way as anyone else — we all see the world differently. The book celebrates famous painters such as Georges Seurat, whose painting *A Sunday on La Grande Jatte* is used to convey that no one sees Sundays like Seurat did.

Once you have read aloud *No One Saw* and shown the pictures, ask students to think of how each person in the class is unique in the stories and interpretations he or she brings to learning. Some teachers take the idea of unique images and create class books featuring self-portraits of every child in the classroom accompanied by positive statements about the child. Others may involve students in writing poetry.

Here are two poems created by two different classes: one Junior, one Intermediate. Note how they expand on the idea "No one sees . . . ," pointing to the uniqueness of the students.

Multiple Ways of Seeing the World
If we can find space in a hurried and crowded curriculum to listen to various interpretations and respect that diversity, then we are well on our way to creating a more inclusive, respectful world.

Junior Class:
No one sees baseball like Erin.
No one sees computers like Nell.
No one sees soccer like Alex.
No one sees ballet like Amy.

No one plays short stop like Erin.
No one clicks the mouse like Nell.
No one scores a goal like Alex.
No one goes up on her toes like Amy.

Erin, go pick up that bat
Nell, get that mouse to chase that cat.
Alex, don't be afraid to pass the ball.
Amy, on your tippitoes, till you fall.

Intermediate Class:
No one sees artwork like Ahmed.
No one sees money like Nick.
No one sees clothes like Shawne.
No one sees cars like Jess.

No one paints canvases like Ahmed.
No one counts pennies like Nick.
No one spends a paycheck like Shawne.
No one buys gas like Jess.

Ahmed, pour that paint.
Nick, you're no saint.
Shawne, dressed to the nines, but broke.
Remember, Jess, cars are for older folk.

Inclusion Practices That Foster Teachers' Evolving Sense of Self

In 2014, I was invited by the Ministry of Education to speak at a conference of Ontario Focused Intervention Partnership, or OFIP, schools. The participants in the conference were the superintendents, principals, and teachers who teach in the lowest-performing schools in the province. The location was a big ballroom in a suburban hotel — and I was nervous about meeting the group and saying the right things about the formidable challenges they faced.

Embrace the challenges

I knew I wanted to encourage these educators to keep going. I wanted to tell them that they were the "superstars" of education — the people who do not give up on the children who present them with many different kinds of challenges. I also wanted to give them an opportunity to think about their teaching in new ways — by revisiting where they had come from, reiterating what their teaching dreams were and are, describing the teaching contexts they faced, and finding ways to move forward that were positive, enlightening, and empowering. I felt that the conference might be a good opportunity for everyone to talk about their teaching practice: to be honest about what might not be working and what they might do differently to make the learning more precise and accountable.

Deputy Minister of Education Mary Jean Gallagher opened the conference. In her keynote address she began by challenging the participants to think about equitable education for all. "There are no disposable children in the world," she said.

The impact of those words on me and on the rest of the audience was palpable. The teachers in the audience understood this principle in their hearts, but every day faced — and face — enormous challenges with students who, for all sorts of complicated reasons, fall below the standards of academic success. Gallagher's words to them served as a call to action — a call to continue working despite the poverty, mental illness, disenchantment, disability, and all sorts of other challenges and difficulties that many of their students face every day.

Critically assess teaching approach and practice

At the conference, I prompted the teachers to spend some time thinking about the students they taught. They worked with their school colleagues after responding to the following questions: "What do I want my classroom to feel like? look like? sound like? What overriding quality do I want to establish from the beginning of the year to the end? How will I get each one of my students to sparkle in a unique way? How will I nurture, support, intrigue, and challenge them to take risks so that they will think critically about things that they are learning and communicate their new knowledge to me and others in exciting and artistic ways? What am I doing that is working? What am I doing that needs to change? What kinds of supports do I need right now to help me make a difference in the lives of these children? To whom can I turn for support? What do I need to read so that I can learn more? How can I take care of myself so that I can take care of my students?" These are questions that all educators must address on their own and with their colleagues, and to do so constantly and honestly.

Equity versus Equality

There needs to be an understanding of the difference between equity and equality. *Equity* speaks to differentiated learning — to teaching and supporting students in ways that will allow them to have equal opportunities. *Equality* means that we teach everyone exactly the same. This approach, however, cannot be the way to take when we know that we have students who did not come into our classrooms with the same starting point. We have to help students in different ways, to teach them with a fair and just outcome in mind.

"There are no disposable children in the world."
— Mary Jean Gallagher

Reflect on teaching experiences

In my teaching experience, successful, inclusive schools evolve when courageous leadership is in place, when teachers collaborate with one another, when the principal values everyone's work, not showing favoritism, when leadership is shared, when students' identities are explicit and honored, when all students are seen as an investment, not as a cost, and when everyone has a vision and a belief in a future filled with high expectations for all learners.

Below I outline one experience that contributed to this understanding.

When I was in my third year of teaching, a new principal arrived at my high school. Bob Brooks was a dynamic leader who advanced many exciting ideas. Unfortunately, he died suddenly over the Christmas holidays, and in the new year, we returned to a school without a principal.

For some reason, the board of education did not replace Bob until the following September, and so from January to June, the staff pitched in to keep the school functioning at a high academic level. The heads of departments shared the leadership, and the school functioned well. I witnessed staff meetings that were organized and respectful, and in which the staff were consulted and their input valued. I watched teachers who had been on the sidelines come forward to serve on committees that enacted changes in the way things had been done in the school for years — they made significant contributions. I was amazed at how exciting it was to teach in a large, urban collegiate setting where everyone's voice mattered.

This is just one of *my* teaching stories — a story that shaped my understanding of what teaching and leading mean in contemporary schools.

We all bring teaching stories with us. These teaching stories are important because, as we tell them, we share who we are, how we teach, what we value, what our strengths are, and how we work with students. Mapping our teaching lives allows us to share what we remember and helps us think about how to forge positive school memories for our students.

Consider the influence of our own experiences as students

Students benefit when teachers understand how their own experiences in schools affect the way that they teach. Because of this, I ask teachers to consider the conditions that they experienced in school and to analyze how these might be similar to or different from those of the students they teach.

In workshops, I ask teachers to find a partner — someone they do not know well — and for the partners to sit back to back. I give each person an index card, lines on one side, blank on the other. I ask them to draw a map on the blank side of the card. They are to include all the landmarks that they remember seeing on the way to an elementary school they attended. They might have taken a school bus or been driven by a parent. Maybe they walked or biked. How they got there does not matter as long as they record what they saw on the way to school. I ask them to label the roads, intersections, places of interest, and so on. The map can be as simple or as detailed as they like.

I then prompt them to turn the card over, to draw a square, leaving space around it, and to write words within the square that describe the feelings and experiences of being in that particular school. These are my questions:
- Once your journey was over and you entered the school building, what was the experience?

- Did you feel included or excluded? honored or dishonored? welcomed or shunned? anonymous or famous? ordinary? bullied? satisfied? challenged? excited? disillusioned? supported? well taught?

I give the teachers a few minutes to write inside the box. Then I ask:
- What were the conditions that allowed you to have this experience in school?
- Why do you think that you had this kind of experience?

Teachers reflect on the context of that particular school and, on the outside of the box, record why they might have had the experience they did.

After they have done this, I encourage the participants to remember their years in school so that their personal school experiences can inform their learning about teaching. We spend time thinking about what made school "work" for them. What was it about the school culture, the teaching, the curriculum, the resources, the extracurricular activities, and the school leadership that allowed them to succeed? We also talk about the barriers to learning. What occurred when the teaching/learning dynamic shut down? Why do they think that happened? What could have been done to prevent it?

After the partners have done their independent work, I ask them to turn to their partner to share how they got to school, how they felt when they got there, what kinds of experiences they had in the school, and what kinds of conditions allowed them to have those experiences.

We conclude by discussing the following questions:
- What do you know?
- Where have you been?
- Where are you from?
- What skills do you have?
- What stories can you tell us about what has brought you here to be with us?
- How can you tap into your many strengths and gifts to help you teach?
- How do you think sharing these stories about your identities and experiences will help all of us teach?

An Exercise in Achieving Insight

One of the most powerful experiences I had doing this exercise took place in a huge, brand-new elementary school outside Toronto, Irma Coulson Public School. The teachers had been working in partners and, after the exercise, we took a break. Two teachers approached me and told me their story. Strangely enough, they had attended the same school but at different times because there was an age difference of about seven years. One teacher had been an English as a Second Language student; the other came from a family that had lived in the area for a few generations.

Their experiences in the school had been entirely different.

One teacher had found learning a new language and adjusting to a new culture almost overwhelming at times. Her experience in school had been challenging. She was lonely and disengaged, and considered an outsider. So, as a teacher, she is well aware of how her immigrant students feel and the kinds of supports they need. She understands their story because of her own experience.

> The other teacher said that hearing this story made her realize how unconscious she had been of other kinds of student experiences in the school. Doing the exercise allowed her to be aware of her own privilege both in school and beyond and to think about the kinds of challenges her students must be facing.

Approaches to Fostering Teachers' Sense of Community

On one occasion, I worked with the staff of Pierre Elliott Trudeau Secondary School in the York Region Board of Education, doing the exercise outlined above. I then asked the teachers to draw a map of the hallways in the school and the roads that led away from the school. I prompted them to consider these questions:

- What are the conditions in that school that are different from the ones that they encountered as secondary school students?
- How are the homes the same or different than they remember?
- Given these contexts and histories, how should we teach differently?
- What do we need to take into account?
- How can we have high expectations but give support to students who might not have the support at home that they need?
- How do our past stories of schools implicate us in the decisions that we make as teachers?

Try to understand what students' lives are like

After we had done this exercise, it became clear to many in the room that the lives of the students we teach are very different from the lives that we lived as students. Today, in a two-parent family, both parents are likely working, and there are many single-parent homes. Most of the students are on their own from the end of the school day to the time a parent arrives home.

Internet access seems to have filled the void. One teacher pointed out that there used to be down time — time away from school and peers, time to kick a soccer ball around, time to do homework without the distraction of Facebook or Twitter, and so on. So, how do we teach students to focus, prioritize, and leave the distractions behind for a while? How do we persuade them to put away the devices so that there can be a quiet time to reflect on life, relationships, patterns, and more?

Act as a stakeholder in the community

If we seriously intend to create inclusive classrooms, we must strive to know and understand the communities in which our students live and to recognize how gender, race, ethnicity, immigrant status, social class, urban/rural context, national origin, sexual orientation, and linguistic backgrounds shape interactions in the classroom. We need to stop and gain information so that we are not seen as tourists in the school community but as people who are part of the wider community and who have an interest and a stake in what is happening there and in our classrooms. In efforts to educate ourselves about the rich diversity of the

---

"Our kids are growing up in a digital playground and no one is on recess duty."
Source: www.edutopia.org/blog/why-kids-should-have-smartphones-matt-levinson?utm_source=twitter&utm_medium=post&utm_campaign=blog-why-kids-smartphones-quote

Chapter 2 explores how teachers can stop, look, and listen to understand who their students are.

students in our classrooms, we need to promote respect for others, encourage close personal relationships, structure effective communication contexts, and imbue in everyone an engaged concern for the common good.

> **Thinking Critically about the Teaching Context**
>
> Much of my thinking about the relationship between teachers and the school community has been affected by Carl James, a colleague at York University, Faculty of Education, who teaches courses on urban education to student teachers. In an article titled "Urban Education: An Approach to Community-Based Education," Carl writes:
>
>> Specifically, I seek to engage teacher-candidates in a process through which they could come to think critically of the contexts in which they teach, recognize the subjectivities they bring to their work with and assumptions of students, and to understand that the attitudes, behaviours, needs, expectations and aspirations of their students are related to the larger social structure in which they/we are all implicated. To this end, through my syllabi and pedagogical approach, I aim to engage teacher-candidates in a process whereby they begin to think about the selves they bring to the teaching-learning process, their understandings of the students' lives and communities, and their development of class curriculum and pedagogical approaches which would make their teaching-learning processes relevant and supportive of the needs, interests and aspirations of their students. (2004, 2)
>
> The approach that Carl outlines is one that teachers who seek to be inclusive in their classrooms are wise to consider.

Reach out to the community

So, how can teachers and principals reach out to the community to promote the sharing of resources? At one school in which I work regularly, the staff meetings are held off-site. Sometimes, they are conducted in the food court in the mall, where the very presence of a large group of teachers buying coffee and sitting in a public space is a powerful experience. Other times, an apartment superintendent will invite the staff into the party room on the first floor of the building. A staff meeting, especially one held within the community, can become a forum where community members are invited to speak.

Sometimes, school, community, and parents may be able to negotiate an agreement to influence how students spend their time outside school for the better. At one meeting where the topic of children arriving home well before their parents was discussed, an apartment owner agreed to establish a supervised space where children could do their homework and be with other children.

Another reason to reach out to the school community is to help ensure that members are aware of a range of pertinent community resources. The school can use social media or flyers sent home with students to transmit this information.

Reaching out may also result in bringing into the school parents or grandparents, or others with artistic skills, as regular visitors, supporting the delivery of arts-based curriculum to many classes.

Assuming Responsibility for the World

To Teach: The Journey of a Teacher was named Book of the Year in 1993 by Kappa Delta Pi and won the Witten Award for Distinguished Work in Biography and Autobiography in 1995.

All effective teachers want the students in their classrooms to feel that they are valued individually as well as collectively. According to William Ayers, author of *To Teach: The Journey of a Teacher*, traditional curriculum design focuses on facts and skills and *assumes* that deeper conceptual understanding occurs. As I have worked on my research project with teachers across Ontario, I have learned that teachers need time to work towards creating deep knowledge, transferable understanding, and higher-order thinking skills among their students. They need to move from procedural to conceptual teaching, where critical analysis is part of the work that occurs every day in classrooms.

There are no easy answers — and the work that occurs is often not about right or wrong answers, but all the grey areas that happen in between. Teachers, therefore, need to be facilitators of learning — "working the room" — challenging ideas and helping students ask questions that have multiple answers.

The experience of effective, transformational teaching is something hard to pin down. Part of it relies on the quality of relationships that teachers have with students, students have with one another and with learning, and teachers and students have to their personal selves. Part of it relies on the kinds of choices that teachers make about how and what to teach. In my work with pre-service teacher candidates, I ask them to think about Hannah Arendt's assertion that "education is the point at which we decide whether we love the world enough to assume responsibility for it."

The Point of Decision

"Education is the point at which we decide whether we love the world enough to assume responsibility for it, and by the same token save it from that ruin which, except for renewal, except for the coming of the new and the young, would be inevitable. And education, too, is where we decide whether we love our children enough not to expel them from our world and leave them to their own devices, nor to strike from their hands their chance of undertaking something new, something unforeseen by us, but to prepare them in advance for the task of renewing a common world."
— Hannah Arendt

Some teacher candidates do not realize how their work is connected to the success of the society in which we live. To further this understanding, I ask them to consider the contexts in which their students live and the ways in which education systems are constructed. In learning how to challenge inequity in education, they need to focus not only on the students they encounter but also on the larger communities from which they come. I ask them to consider the difficulties faced by families and to challenge the economic and political obstacles that many families face in their communities. The work of teachers, I tell them, is to empower everyone within and outside the classroom.

A teacher's job is to look after *everyone* in the classroom: to be aware of who is contributing and who is not, who is engaged and who is drifting away. The teacher has to know how to reel in those individuals who feel disempowered and to work well with the class as a collective. The effective teacher knows who is there, how each student got there, what she or he is ready to accomplish, and how to help everyone despite the challenges that anyone might be facing.

No small order.

2

Stop, Look, and Listen — Identity

Part of a Performance Piece: Nish Students
Know this about us:

That we want to learn and we want to go far.
We want to learn and we want to go far.
We want to succeed.
School is important so — therefore — YOU are important.
— Mnjikaning Kendaaswin Elementary School, Rama, Ontario

Teaching and learning are dynamic processes. They require imagination, a developed sense of timing, an understanding of the prior knowledge of students, information about how to make accommodations and modifications for those students who need them, careful consideration of space, experience in making transitions from one activity to the other, and creative management of materials. They also demand an excitement about the path ahead and a flexibility to change gears before and during the lesson. The goal is to make learning experiences as powerful and as transformational as possible.

One cannot begin to plan, however, unless one has an understanding about who is in the room. I live and teach in Toronto — one of the most diverse cities in the world. There are enormous opportunities and specific challenges associated with teaching in schools that have such complex and varied student populations. I work with teachers and teacher candidates, helping them find ways to eliminate bias, prevent discrimination, and maintain high expectations of excellence for every student in their classrooms. I also work with administrators who share with me their vision of an "inclusive school," where all students have opportunities to succeed and to go into the world prepared to live life to the fullest.

The Equity Agenda as Journey

"If school is about preparing students for active citizenship, what better citizenship tool than to critically analyze the society?"
— Gloria Ladson-Billings, "But That's Just Good Teaching! The Case for Culturally Relevant Pedagogy," *Theory into Practice*, page 162

For the past few years, I have had the privilege of working with teachers and principals to help them find ways of anchoring culturally responsive and relevant pedagogy into the working fabric of their schools. The three ideas that underpin culturally responsive and relevant pedagogy are as follows:

1. Students learn what is most meaningful to them.
2. Students' diverse locations and identities are explored collectively and are used as vehicles for learning.
3. Students and teachers are encouraged to be critical of inequality, bias, and discrimination on all sorts of levels. Students learn how to critique cultural norms, values, mores, and institutions that produce and maintain social inequities. They become aware of what is unfair not just for themselves but for others.

The challenge is always to include everyone in these difficult conversations and to ensure that the work is connected to students' personal success and academic achievement. In workshops and seminars, teachers and I spend time together redefining what *inclusive curriculum* is, imagining schools where every student is successful, finding ways to welcome parents and members of the school community into the learning experience, looking at our own biases and assumptions, finding out how to get to know who our students are and where they are from, and understanding that high expectations for all students must be supported by sufficient time, academic preparation, and varied resources.

School leaders hope that their staff members will find personal connections and professional relevance to social justice so that there will be equity for all. The teacher's job in public education has always been about fairness. As we teach, we are intent on eliminating bias, preventing discrimination, and maintaining high expectations of excellence for every student. Why do we strive so hard to make sure that teaching works and that learning matters? Because we want our students to get caught up in the full current of life — both in school and beyond — and to make good choices for the future. We want them to lead lives that are privately happy and publicly useful. We want them to grasp on to hope as they grow and learn despite the difficulties in their paths.

Teachers make an enormous difference in the lives of students simply on the basis of how and what they teach. We need to be aware of what many equity educators call the "location" of our students in terms of their identities and to work with curriculum that is responsive to their needs and interests. We must also strive to know and understand the communities in which our students live and to recognize how gender, race, ethnicity, immigrant status, social class, urban/rural context, national origin, sexual orientation, and linguistic backgrounds shape interactions in the classroom. Finally, it is crucial for teachers to unpack their own stories of identity and to be aware of how their privilege and power influence the classroom dynamic.

Equity is a key component in education. As the Ontario Ministry of Education (2009, 5) put it in *Realizing the Promise of Diversity*: "To improve outcomes for students at risk, all partners must work to identify and remove barriers and must actively seek to create the conditions needed for student success. . . . that means ensuring that all of our students are engaged, included, and respected, and that they see themselves reflected in their learning environment."

When invited to work with school teams, I outline several approaches and entry points to this challenging work. I know, however, that I need to rely upon school leaders to introduce this critically important work to their staffs and to set the context for the journey that lies ahead.

The equity agenda in education has often been described as a journey, so it is not unusual for me to begin my first session with a group of teachers by prompting them to think about the words that any good crossing guard teaches students who are about to cross the street. I ask them to stop, look, and listen.

Stop to Take Stock

When leading workshops to encourage fairness and equity, I invite everyone in the room to "stop" so that we can take stock of who we are and why we are present. Participants, who often have a wide range of experiences as teachers, are given the opportunity to remember why they became educators in the first place.

I begin by posting quotations that speak to different ways of living and learning in the world. After the quotations are up throughout the workshop space, I invite my colleagues to walk around the room alone, examining the quotations. I tell them to find the quotation that interests them, disturbs them, inspires them, or connects with them the most.

Here are some of the quotations I post:

> As I listen to what participants say to their partner, in small groups, or to the entire group, I find out a bit about the thoughts and feelings of the people in the room — why they stay in teaching, what theories influenced them, what keeps them motivated, what they long for, and what they hope to achieve.

A Sampling of Quotations to Stand By

"Words are humanity's greatest natural resource, but most of us have trouble figuring out how to put them together. Words aren't cheap. They are very precious. They are like water, which gives life and growth and refreshment, but because it has always been abundant, we treat it cheaply. We waste it; we pollute it, and doctor it. Later we blame the quality of the water because we have misused it."
— Katherine Paterson

"The children who need recess the most are the first ones to lose it. Being removed from field trips, the cafeteria, library and all other learning opportunities only makes students less able to handle them in the future. No one would say to a basketball player, 'You missed too many foul shots. You can't practice until you get better.' It is time to stop giving more opportunities to those who have already proven they are successful while denying opportunities to those who need them the most." — Richard Curwin

"Believing in students is not simply telling them that you believe in them. These words matter only if they are true and if you demonstrate them by your actions. There is no way to fake it, because kids have built in crap detectors and they can tell if you don't mean it."
— Neil Postman and Charles Weingartner

"A shy teacher may compare herself with another colleague and think, 'I should be more dynamic and outspoken like her.' However, the shy teacher who is quiet and gentle in her manner may provide students who are surrounded by dynamic and flamboyant people with a model of someone who is quieter, does not rush in to speak first, etc. This may be a tremendous affirmation that it is OK to be shy and gentle for students who need to see that reflected in someone in a position of authority."
— B. J. Richmond

"The teacher must then cope not only with the reality of teaching, which may be difficult enough, but also with these inner voices of super-idealism and guilt. These myths are true fantasies.... They sap the teacher's inner strengths by weakening his self-confidence and denying the uniqueness of each teacher as a separate, special human being."   — Herbert M. Greenberg

"To believe in a child is to believe in the future. Through their aspirations they will save the world. With their combined knowledge the turbulent seas of hate and injustice will be calmed. They will champion the causes of life's underdogs, forging a society without class discrimination. They will supply humanity with music and beauty as it has never known. They will endure. Towards these ends I pledge my life's work. I will supply the children with tools and knowledge to overcome the obstacles. I will pass on the wisdom of my years and temper it with patience. I shall impact in each child the desire to fulfill his or her dream. I shall teach."   — Henry James

"Education signifies an initiation into new ways of seeing, hearing, feeling, moving. It signifies the nurture of a special kind of reflectiveness and expressiveness, a reaching out for meanings, a learning to learn."   — Maxine Greene

"No one has realized the wealth of sympathy, the kindness and generosity hidden in the soul of a child. The effort of every true education should be to unlock that treasure."   — Emma Goldman

> "Change is inevitable; transformation is possible."
> — Penny Milton, *Shifting Minds 3.0: Redefining the Learning Landscape in Canada*, page 6

> Emily Style and Peggy McIntosh are associated with SEED, which is an acronym for Seeking Educational Equity & Diversity. It is a national project on inclusive curriculum, based in the United States.

Teachers stand by their choice and discuss it with the others who made the same choice. They then read the quotation out loud and report the key points of their small-group discussion to the larger group.

The teachers and I continue to talk about what we are teaching, how we are teaching it, to whom we are teaching it, and under what conditions. Participants share how their teaching lives have changed, as 21st century classrooms demand a more multi-faceted perspective and different approaches. We focus on content, pedagogy, access, and climate.

Ten questions: Curriculum as window and mirror

We then ask ourselves 10 key questions and discuss them. Question #8 uses imagery adopted by Emily Style and Peggy McIntosh. According to these researchers, curriculum is an architectural structure that schools build around students. Style's metaphor of curriculum as window and mirror complements McIntosh's concern for multiple perspectives in education and embodies a view of school curriculum that provides students with opportunities to see not only the realities of others (curriculum as window) but also the representations of their own realities (curriculum as mirror).

If the student is understood as occupying a dwelling of self, then education needs to enable the student to look through window frames in order to see the realities of others and into mirrors in order to see her or his own reality reflected. When curriculum is viewed in this way, differences as well as similarities are validated, and students' understanding of themselves in relation to others is expanded.

Here are my 10 questions:

1. What are our particular challenges?
2. How effective are we at making sure that all students are being included?
3. What are the conditions that allow students to succeed?
4. Which conditions that are in place block students from being successful?
5. What are we doing about the unevenness of program delivery and student success?
6. Who gets "privileged" and why?
7. How might we open multiple windows on the world so that our students learn from various perspectives and in different dimensions?
8. How can we find ways to have the curriculum act like a mirror — so that students see the diversity and complexity of their varied backgrounds and personal experiences reflected back to them?
9. What new teaching strategies and approaches can we devise and use so that students are actively engaged with others in co-constructing their understanding of the content in multiple ways?
10. Who and what is getting in the way of engaged, effective teaching?

This exercise is an important one for teachers and leaders to complete because it helps them define what inclusive curriculum could mean for them personally.

Reflecting and affirming diversity: A vision

I share my vision with them. For me, inclusive curriculum is an approach to teaching and learning that recognizes and values the rich diversity of our teachers, our students, our communities, and the global population. Its goal is to create learning environments that reflect, affirm, celebrate, and validate the diversity and complexity of the human experience. Honoring the diversity that lies before us does not, however, mean lowering our expectations. Lisa Delpit (1996) reminds us about the importance of maintaining "high academic press" for all students at the same time, ensuring that these high expectations are complemented and supported by sufficient resources.

So, this first "stop" on the journey towards understanding our role in constructing inclusive curriculum begins where people are.

Look in Multiple Ways

The second part of the journey across the intersection focuses on looking at our students and the environments that shape them.

Crossing guards have often directed children to "look both ways before crossing the street." In 21st century classrooms this approach is not nearly sufficient. Most of us are serving a much more diverse student population, so it becomes incumbent upon us to look at our students, curriculum, communities, and classrooms in multiple ways. We need to train our eyes to notice things we might not have seen before — to look at our students from various vantage points, to take time to wonder about their strengths, to notice their challenges, to honor their intelligences, to find their hidden talents, to research their "location," and to celebrate their identities.

Look at the school environment

We look at the learning environments, as well — not just the classroom but also all areas of the school. In my workshops, I invite the teachers to use their imaginations to enter various rooms in the schools where they teach. We ask ourselves critical questions about the appearance, content, use, and access associated with those rooms. For example:
- Is there a wide variety of food available in the cafeteria that reflects students' cultures and identities?
- Are the signs, notices, posters, motivational comments, and displays in the school building multilingual, and do they reflect a variety of cultural perspectives?
- Is there a private place where students can pray if they wish to?
- How are parents or guardians welcomed when they come to the main office? Are translation services available for those families that do not speak English?

Look into the school community

We also talk about the need to look beyond the school walls and to venture out into the school community. One formal initiative that explored this is the School Community Engaged Education (SCEE) Project, based at Toronto's York University and in partnership with the Toronto District School Board. The project focused on knowing and understanding the communities in which students live. Teachers who were part of it were encouraged not to be seen as "tourists" (Solomon and Levine-Rasky 2007, 21) in the community in which they teach, but as people with a stake in what is happening there and in their classrooms. Participants were also encouraged to look at their students in terms of the whole child and to understand and honor every child's traditions, culture, experiences, and realities so that they could plan curriculum events and learning opportunities to help the students succeed.

Look within ourselves and the system of education

In *Shifting Minds 3.0*, her report on 21st century change in education, Penny Milton advocates for a shift away from hierarchical policy-driven systems towards networks of strong, responsive schools, with educators collaborating continuously and sharing knowledge both horizontally and vertically.

"In these transformed systems, leaders at the top empower leadership at all levels, resulting in schools and classrooms that are holistic and adaptive," she writes. "The dual strategies of school improvement and innovation work together to hold the system in balance so that all parts of the whole can adapt without spinning out of control" (2015, 7).

Equity is at the heart of the work, and the time spent looking for something that is or is not directly apparent is an essential part of the work in schools. This kind of "looking," however, makes us recognize that we bring our own biases, assumptions, and expectations into the mix. I think we would all agree that sometimes it is easier to look the other way and not acknowledge race, gender, class, and power in our teaching lives. But this acknowledgment is a fundamental part of teaching fairly in an unfair world.

In a course on urban diversity taught in the Faculty of Education at York University in Toronto, Carl James (2004, 3) encourages his teacher candidates to recognize that the racism inherent in educational structures must be labeled and addressed directly: "Critical educators make explicit the contradictions and paradoxes that are inherent in institutions, such as schools, which promise equality and inclusivity while producing and reproducing inequalities based on race, class, gender and other factors."

Listen to Voices Silent and Heard

Listening is an act of social justice. Part of our task is to pay attention to the ways in which we talk to each other and to our students in classrooms, labs, hallways, cafeterias, dance studios, gymnasia, and soccer fields. Words can be key mechanisms for both oppression and for transformation. It is important to learn to be mindful of the power of language. Consider these words from *Teacher and Child: A Book for Parents and Teachers* by Haim Ginott (1972, 67):

> I have come to a frightening conclusion. I am the decisive element in the classroom. It is my personal approach that creates the climate. It is my daily mood that makes the weather. As a teacher, I possess tremendous power to make a child's life joyous. I can be a tool for torture or an instrument of inspiration. I can humiliate or humour; hurt or heal. In all situations it is my response that decides whether a crisis will be escalated or de-escalated, a child humanized or de-humanized.

At last, we are on the final part of the journey across the intersection. This is where the workshops become more challenging and where the crucial aspect of courageous, collaborative leadership comes to the fore. It is essential to ensure that the work regarding teacher and student voice is safe, respectful, and professional. I help participants recognize that the way the dominant culture maintains its position often happens without people being aware of how it does so. Because our personal and professional identities shape the way we see our work, we must be mindful of how privilege and power influence the classroom dynamic — how assumptions hide truths and how power silences those who, for various reasons, have been shunned.

No doubt, we have spent lots of time hearing those confident student voices that are regularly present in our classrooms; we now need to listen for the silent voices — to find room for them, to let them speak for the first time. So, who are the students with silent voices? Among others, they are the English Language Learners (ELLs), the children who are bullied or ostracized, and the students who are afraid that they are not as smart as everyone else and so remain silent. We also need to ask ourselves why these students have not been heard until now and to be critically aware of systemic injustice and how this has made them feel.

It is far easier for us to not notice these students — to not probe, to not wait, to keep the momentum up by not stopping and listening for someone to share ideas. All teachers, including me, need to remind themselves that not everyone enters the classroom with ease. Many students are anxious about how they come across and need to know that the teacher is aware of them and is in their corner.

In one school that participated in the *All I's on Education* project, a teacher, Beth Renaud, remembered being the child in school whom the teacher never noticed. This experience of being ignored as a young student now affects the way that she teaches. Here is what she said about the students she notices because they remind her of herself:

> I see them in my class, trying to fly under the radar — too shy, too awkward, too unsure, too scared — the ones whose heads are filled with so many other worries that what I have to say about my lessons really doesn't hold a candle to the things that occupy their thoughts. I see them in my classroom trying to avoid making eye contact. They aren't looking for great acts of kindness. They just want — no, they need — to be acknowledged that they are there, present. I know that they are yearning to find their place in my class. And it's my goal to acknowledge that yearning — to make sure they feel wanted, appreciated, and accepted here — not just once in a while, but every single day. It's what drives me to be the teacher that I am: helping my students to find their own joy of learning, their own particular, unique voices.

Start with a Person's Name

When I was teaching a course at the University of Victoria, one student told the story of teachers always mispronouncing her name — all through school. Sonia Manak was also the only South Asian student throughout her time in school. She felt intimidated and did not think that she could insist that people learn to say her name correctly. She had always remained silent; however, when I asked everyone to learn each other's names on the first day of the course, she felt empowered to tell her story.

> At the end of the class, another student, Taylor Caswell, wrote and performed a song about her story. Here are the lyrics.
>
> My name has meaning
> and the word you use instead has meaning too
> 'cause every time that you don't see
> that the "i" in my name isn't silent like me
> you take my identity
> and run it over.
>
> You run me over.
>
> How can you help me
> when you don't know me?
> And you don't know me.
> So let me ask:
> Is who I am worth your time?
> Is who I am worth your time?
> Then learn my name.
> Learn my real name.
> Learn my name.
> We can start with my name.

Becoming Part of a Movement

Young people on the way to and from school expect that the crossing guards at busy intersections will help them cross safely to the other side of the street. What's more, students enter school expecting that the adults who are entrusted with their care will work on their behalf for their personal and academic success. Teachers thus have a purpose somewhat similar to that of crossing guards: to make students safe and help them navigate the unfinished journey towards democracy and social justice in education. They can protect students into understanding by encouraging them to stop, look, and listen.

By taking the time to do this important work, all of us can be part of a movement that will establish schools as places where there is respect, not just tolerance; where there is community, not just group process; where there are relationships, not just connections; and where empathy and compassion are based on mutual understanding, not on superficial encounters.

Games That Promote Identity

Researchers Peggy McIntosh and Emily Style have helped me realize that teachers and students need to talk about who they are, get to know one another, and acknowledge "the textbooks of their lives." Storytelling allows us to get to know one another, to have informed conversations about who we are, where we are from, and what we want to achieve individually as well as collectively.

The following exercises encourage students to spend time getting to know one another — finding out each other's names, learning about where everyone comes from, and having a chance to play games so that there is laughter, engagement, and activity. Name games are an important way to begin. They allow students not only to learn each other's names but also how to pronounce the names, remember them, and build a kind of collective awareness of the classroom community.

Say Your Name

Students stand in a circle. Each says his or her name, one after the other. When students do it again, the teacher asks them to say their name loudly, then in whispers right after. Then, when a student says her or his name, everyone repeats the name. In this way, the student helps the class learn how to pronounce the name correctly.

Ball Throw

This game is played when the students already know one another's names.

Have students walk to the empty spaces in the room. Throw a ball up in the air and call a student's name. That student tries to catch it. Once the student has it, he or she calls another person's name. The game continues until all names have been called.

The Seat on My Right Is Free

Have the students sit in a circle on chairs. Make sure that there is one empty chair. The person to the left of the empty chair says: "The seat on my right is free. I would like to invite [someone in the class] to sit beside me." The person who is invited crosses the circle, which frees up a chair. The game continues with the person to the left of the empty chair repeating: "The seat on my right is free. I would like to invite _____ to sit beside me." Make these two rules: everyone is to receive an invitation, and no person can be invited more than once.

Name Switch Now

Students stand in a circle. One person is "It." "It" establishes eye contact with someone across the circle and then says his or her own name and the name of the other person. "It" begins to walk towards this person, who establishes eye contact with another, says his or her own name and the name of the other, and begins walking towards that person. They switch places. The game should be played quickly, and everyone should have a turn. Encourage students to "give each other their eyes" as they say their names and somebody else's.

Name Call Ball Toss

Students stand in a circle. To begin, a ball is given to one player, who calls his or her name and tosses the ball to someone else in the circle. The ball continues to be passed, ensuring that all become familiar with the names in the group.

The activity is repeated. This time, students begin with their hands folded in front of them; after tossing the ball to someone else in the circle, students place their hands behind their backs. In this way, each person passes and receives the ball once.

The activity is repeated again. Draw the students' attention to the pattern that has been established.

Extensions
- Challenge the students to complete the activity within a time limit.
- Students pass the ball in the same pattern. Names are not called.
- The pattern of passing the ball is reversed. The ball is passed from the last person to the first person.
- Two balls are passed, one using the original pattern and one using the reverse pattern.
- Up to five additional balls are added.

Ball Game with Words and Phrases

Students choose a slip of paper from an envelope that contains a word or phrase from a text they have been studying. The word or phrase that they select will be their personal word or phrase and they need to "own" it and memorize it.

Students stand in a circle. One person is handed a ball and tosses it to someone else in the circle. That person calls out the "owned" word or phrase. The game continues until everyone has had a chance to receive the ball, say aloud the chosen word, and throw the ball to someone else.

The activity is repeated, and students are asked to add an emotional dimension to the word or phrase.

Extension

Students work in groups of three to five. They create a short scene in which everyone says his or her word or phrase from the ball exercise. They decide on the order of lines and create appropriate gestures and emotions to enhance the meaning behind the words. Various interpretations of the lines are encouraged and expected.

My Name Has Meaning

Behind every name is a story. To begin, students can turn to one or two classmates to tell a story about their name. The following questions can be used to guide the discussion:
- Why did their parents choose to give them this name?
- What does their name mean?
- Do they have a nickname?
- Do they like their name? Why or why not?
- Do they know their name in other another language? If so, what is it?
- If they had a chance to choose another name, what would that be? Why?
- Do they have more than one name? If so, are they willing to share their other given names with the class? What are the names?

Students may decide to convert their oral name stories into writing in order to share them with others. Suggest that each student add a picture or a name crest to the piece of writing. The name stories could be collated into a take-home book called "Our Name Stories" and then shared with students' families.

> **Sharing Name Stories**
>
> I once delivered a workshop on name stories with a large group of secondary and elementary school students in a location close to my university. The secondary school students came from four high schools where there was a fair amount of rivalry and considerable tension among the school student populations.
>
> One of the secondary school students pulled me aside before the workshop. He said that I needed to know that the students would not work together across school boundaries. "It's just too dangerous," he told me. There were 16 secondary students and 24 Grade 4 students from six of the feeder schools. I weighed what this student said to me and then took a chance.
>
> I divided the groups into four so that schools were mixed — boys and girls, elementary and secondary — a random jumble of bodies in a cafeteria on a muggy May morning. I asked the secondary school students to interview the elementary school students about their names. The sweetness of the stories just melted the secondary school students' hearts so that when it came time to tell their name stories, they did so with a fair amount of generosity and openness. One boy spoke about how his father had been shot to death when his mother was pregnant with him so that he now bears his father's name. I could tell that this story affected everyone in the room.
>
> At the end of the workshop, the same student who had approached me at the beginning came to thank me for the experience. He said he had never participated in a cross-grade, cross-panel workshop before.
>
> "You know," he said. "I was thinking that if we had had this kind of experience when we were in elementary school, we would not have the kinds of tensions that we have now. The rivalry is really scary, and we have to keep to ourselves. Today I learned something about a guy across the territory and it really has affected me, changed me. So thank you for having us share our name stories."

From I to We

This creative activity asks students to examine the kinds of experiences, places, people, words, images, food, sayings, and readings that have shaped who they are. Students write about these things in a structured format and then share their writing with the rest of the class in performance. The idea is drawn from a writing exercise developed by Linda Christensen (2000) in *Reading, Writing, Rising Up: Teaching about Social Justice and the Power of the Written Word*. I have, however, turned her exercise into a performance activity that often results in teachers and others, including parents, hearing a powerful reflection of students' identities expressed in creative ways.

Here is the process I developed.

I hand out a lined index card to each student. They work independently. I say: "This exercise is going to help you write about who you are and what kinds of memories and events have shaped you. I am going to ask you to think about all sorts of things, people, events, and places that are part of your life. I will be asking that you roam all over the place in your imaginations and in your memories. You can record anything that you think you would like to share about yourself. You will have a fair bit of time to write, and then you will have a chance to share your writing with a partner."

I ask the students to find a partner and a pen. They sit back to back with their partners. I direct them to write three words at the top of their index cards: *I Am From*.

Responding to prompts

I then ask students to listen to the prompts I am going to suggest and to respond in writing as spontaneously as they can. The first lot of prompts, below, are relatively simple and straightforward:

I Am From
- a favorite thing to eat (I am from macaroni and cheese fresh out of the oven with breadcrumbs on top)
- landmarks you pass on your way to school or work every day (I am from the gas station at the corner of Elm and Queen streets)
- a favorite family saying, which can be written in your first language (Enough is a feast)
- a keepsake that you will never throw away and the place where you keep it (I am from a photograph of me and my grandmother that I keep in my bedside table drawer)
- a decision that you made or one that was made for you that changed your life forever (I am from coming to Canada when I was nine years old)
- an obstacle that has challenged you to think about your life in new ways (I am from making the decision to quit my hockey team and take art classes instead)
- the way that you are seen by others (I am from "She is good at math and makes friends easily")
- the way that you see yourself (I am from worrying about my brother who is struggling with mental illness)
- a place that you wish you could return to when you have more time and money (I am from the hot beaches of Trinidad)

I then ask the students to revisit what they have written and add some detail, for example: "I am from a photograph of me and my grandmother. A special memory of our last time together. I feel her arms on my shoulders and hear her last words of goodbye." Once they begin composing their individual poems, they can choose the specific responses to prompts they want to include in their final pieces.

Below I have provided a second lot of prompts, somewhat more sophisticated than the first, as well as sample responses:

- your favorite season (I am from Spring . . . where the blossoms in my garden blanket the lawn in whispers)
- an activity you love to do (I am from snowboarding, leaping down mountains in a rush of white)
- something you made or wrote (I am from my poem about my grandfather that I keep in my wallet)

- a goodbye that affected you (I am from my father's hands on my shoulders saying goodbye in Uganda)
- things you collect (I am from old guitars and other musical instruments that I stash in the back of the garage)
- a moment when you felt most alive (I am from skydiving with my sister, my mother watching on the ground with a hand over her mouth)
- a superpower that you wish you had (I am from seeing into people's hearts to know what they are really feeling)
- a real or imagined safe place (I am from sitting alone in my room, with my cat on my lap, listening to my mom starting the BBQ)
- what scares you the most (I am from standing in front of an audience, being expected to say something about myself)
- rules that you try to abide by (I am from showing up on time at work, no matter how tired I am)

Discovering where we are from

Once students have written their responses, I ask them to turn and read what they have just drafted to a partner. They share their writing. I then ask the following questions:
- What do you have in common?
- How are you different?
- What surprised you about your partner?
- Why is it important to be aware of our similarities and differences?

Experimenting with lines for dramatic impact

I then ask the students to combine the lines from both their responses into a common "We Are From" poem. Together, they decide what to change, delete, add, or repeat. Once they have created their poem, I ask them to find a way of reading it out loud so that it has dramatic impact. They play around with solo and duo readings, read their script in whispers, use physical actions, and so on.

Here is the procedure we follow.

1. Students stand face to face. One person holds the poem and reads it aloud to his or her partner. The partner then reads the poem out loud, too. Pairs talk about what changes need to be made and make them.
2. I ask the partners to stand side by side. One of the students holds the poem, which might be on a card, and the students read the poem in unison. I ask them to talk about how the poem sounded when read by two voices.
3. I ask one student to read the first line, the other student to read the second line, and for them to alternate lines until they get to the end of the poem. They keep reading the poem over and over again until I say "Stop." I ask the students to make changes: to add words or phrases that could make the reading of the poem sound better.
4. Next, I ask students to consider what words or phrases might be repeated. They experiment with doing that and make changes on the card.
5. The students are invited to read the poem with anger, in whispers, with joy, and with sadness. I ask them to find their favorite word or phrase in the poem and underline it.

6. I give students about 15 minutes to practice the reading of the poem, incorporating these ideas into the rehearsal process. When they are ready, students share their prepared reading with the rest of the class.

Combining favorite lines

The students are prompted to find their favorite line. We stand in a circle and say these lines and then together find an order of reading that works artistically and theatrically. At the University of Victoria, for example, partners created 11 group poems and then the class developed a final collective poem, included at the end of this section. Two of the group poems follow.

Group 4:
We are from . . .
Neighborhoods where both young and old play;
Where the little corner store is buzzing,
Where we enjoy butter chicken and Grandma's cauliflower casseroles,
Love,
We are put on this earth to walk each other home,
Both negative and positive decisions:
Irresponsible and promiscuous youth-hoods,
And the choices made to be here in this room,
Scrapbooks and security blankets,
Those we look up to, who taught us healing, provided guidance and shared their time and wisdom:
My friend Darlene, my father,
Places where dance can be a celebration of life: Africa, Home.

We are from . . .
Places where we feel safe and places we are loved.

Group 11:
We are from . . .
Winding roads that pass through 4 lane intersections,
Cacophony and finding peace in a quiet green oasis covered in pink blossoms.

We are from . . .
The mix of spices and flavours found in mom's curry chicken,
Jaidi gull licky howia chi honia,
And shut up and use some elbow grease.

We are from . . .
Research to follow our highest heart come hell or high water!
From mothers,
From beloved necklaces left behind,
And cherished safely kept collections of baby teeth.

We are from . . .
Steadfast and strong-willed feisty courage with a vision for justice,
From the well-worn path of spiritual roots and cultural richness.

Every Student with a Voice

Merrill Mathews, principal of Irma Coulson Public School in the Halton District School Board, invited me into his school to see how the entire school population engaged with the "I Am From" exercise. Bulletin boards were full of class poems and on the day that the school officially opened, there was a school-wide performance where every student had a voice, and the audience could see and hear where everyone was from.

The principal affirmed: "This was the perfect activity for our students to celebrate their diversity as our strength and a great reminder that we must take the time to learn each other's story. As a school community, we are driven to ensure that every child knows they belong, and this activity provided us with an opportunity to know each of our students in a very meaningful way."

I Am *Now* From . . .

Another idea is to begin the school year with "I am from . . ." and then at the end of the year, have students create a different poem: "I am *now* from . . ."

The final collective performance piece, which drew on all 11 group poems, went like this:

This is where we are from . . .
We are from . . .
The choice,
The search to follow our highest heart come hell or high water.

We are from . . .
The rhythm of the beach that dances with abandon,
The talking waves,
The silent talk,
Where the sun, sand, and water all meet.

We are from . . .
Grandfather's watches, Tin Boxes, and Bear Skins,
Step outside the Box,
Walk each other home.

Our baggage carried, inked with blue independence
Sure that's life,
You are the one.

How we are from water

For the *All I's on Education* project, referred to earlier, one teacher, Erin Walsh, worked with her Grade 8 students to conduct an inquiry-based project on water. She provided them with 11 prompts, including "a time I've seen/experienced water being used in a ceremony or ritual," "a time when I was immersed in water; where I was and how I felt," and "something water would like to say to us."

Erin helped the students prepare for the culminating event by having them rehearse a choral reading. Students explored the meaning of what they had collectively written by reading the poem aloud in many different ways. They experimented with tempo, tone, pace, repetition, volume, emotion, and different kinds of groupings such as solo, duet, trio, and whole group. They focused their attention on words, language patterns, and punctuation.

In the time spent on finding meaning and powerful dramatic effect, students revisited the text many times. They helped one another and shared ideas. A further benefit was to struggling readers. Because they were blending their voices with those of students who were more fluent, these readers gained confidence in oral language response and in reading out loud.

Here is the final poem that the students of Class 8-1 presented as a choral reading at the culminating event with parents and the community.

WE ARE FROM WATER

We are from water . . .
From a pipeline a vein that runs from Lake Ontario to Milton.
We are from water all around but not a drop to drink, from its liberating momentum
From boiling water to being able to drink it, and working hard every day to retrieve it;
We are from the sweat of women.

We are from thirst; from running the beep test, skating on the pond
and jumping off the dock;
We are from ritual, from baptism, purifying before prayers, and from
the water that comes from Mecca.
We are from the thrill of sailing, from the first time ice-skating to
canoeing at the cottage, from Silent Lake to Niagara Falls, the Great
Barrier Reef to South Africa's rivers, from the Mill Pond.
We are from water going up my nose, and the taste of salt water, from
letting go, surrounded by thoughts;
We are from troubles floating away
From graceful calm sounds, from waves crashing the rocks, from the
freedom of driving a boat, from surfing and belly flops
We are from the depths of the unknown, the lurking, the feel of
something touch my leg to clear, refreshing peaceful beauty
We are from a beautiful source of life and endless injustice, from
water as a right . . .
For all? For some?
We are from Water.

And Everyone's Voice Was Strong

Some years ago, I was privileged to work with Judy Blaney, a course director at York University, and her pre-service teacher candidates from the First Nation, Métis & Inuit Infusion teacher education program at its off-campus site in Barrie, Ontario. The program focuses on the traditions, perspectives, and cultures of Indigenous peoples in Canada, and current and historical issues related to them. The teacher education program is unlike other teacher education programs in Canada because it focuses on infusing an awareness of Indigenous peoples across the entire pre-service curriculum, giving teacher candidates a deeper understanding of relationships in order to bring culturally responsive and responsible programming to all students in Ontario classrooms.

The student teachers were to meet with the students from Mnjikaning Kendaaswin Elementary School in Rama, Ontario. The purpose of the day was for the FNMI students to advise the teacher candidates on how to teach in FNMI community schools. (The student teachers were to spend two weeks in practicum placements in various communities throughout the province.)

The most beautiful thing

I had worked for a few days with Judy and the students. They had spoken about how important it was for teachers to "walk us through" the school experience. We worked with George Littlefield's *What's the Most Beautiful Thing You Know about Horses?* After we had read the book, I asked the students to write on a piece of paper the most beautiful thing, the most surprising thing, the most hidden thing, the most essential thing about themselves, and so on. They each chose the line that they wanted to share, and then we began to weave the poem together. I wanted them to perform the piece, but I knew that they would have to look strong so I taught them how to use Readers Theatre.

The students worked as a class. There was a wide range of reading abilities. One boy told me that he could not read at all. I helped him find his cue as the

---

The Strategy of Readers Theatre
Readers Theatre relies on the power of the words and the skill of groups of readers to fully engage an audience in listening to a text. It
- gives students an authentic reason to engage in repeated reading of texts
- benefits readers who are unsure of their reading
- helps students attend to the meaning in the material they are reading
- involves students in a positive, interactive, social reading activity in which risk taking, experimentation, modeling, instruction, and feedback are natural components of rehearsals

See the description of the strategy in Chapter 5.

students read the text many times in different ways. The readers were drawn into the work as they were needed to speak in unison, make sound effects with their voices, repeat words or phrases, or read the part of a solo character.

Readers Theatre was a perfect vehicle because the students did not have to memorize their parts. They could hold their scripts. We rehearsed the piece many times so that their performance was fluid. I watched as the readers gained confidence, experimenting with ideas, trying the script in different ways, and adjusting roles so that everyone's voice was strong.

On the day of the meeting with the pre-service teacher candidates and the Ontario Education Leadership Camp in Rama, Ontario, the FNMI students stood and read aloud:

What's the most beautiful thing that we know about us?
First and foremost we are Nish. Do you know what that means?
Don't be afraid to ask us questions if you don't know something. We are here to teach and we have lots to tell you about ourselves.
For instance:
The most important thing about me is my language. This is how I say my name in Ojibway.
Would you like to hear all of us say our names?
Here we go:
[And the students said all of their names.]

The most hidden thing about me is that I am quiet and deep. (You might think that I have nothing to say — but wait and listen — my words will find their way to you.)

The most essential thing to me is that I am a good hunter. I have been taught well and I know the land — Look around you. See its beauty. Know that it is at risk.

UMMM . . . What can I tell you about me? I love pizza — oh! And I have a really good sense of humour! (I can make anyone smile!)
We are all connected to our culture, our stories, our language, our family, our relationships, our community and our friends.

We love and honour:

Our UNIQUE LANGUAGE,

THE GRANDFATHER TEACHINGS,
Wisdom, love, honesty, humility, respect, courage and truth

DELICIOUS scones that my granny makes for us.

OUR TRADITIONAL FOODS

And

OUR MEDICINES THAT HEAL US WHEN WE ARE SICK.

Let's not forget the
DRUMS,
OUR REGALIA,
THE POW WOW
THE SWEAT LODGE

THE TIPI AND WIGWAM
FASTING
SPEARING
AND HUNTING.

Know this about us:

That we want to learn and we want to go far.
We want to learn and we want to go far.
We want to succeed.
School is important so — therefore — YOU are important.

We are Nish. We are Ojibway. We are your students. Listen to us so that you can teach us well.

The Potential for a New Kind of Self

As this poem points to, both teachers and students need to be able to collaborate, to have the confidence to take risks, and to share information about their identities and personal stories or journeys so that their gifts, talents, resources, and skills can be utilized by all.

By engaging in the kinds of activities described in this book, students gain self-awareness and a new sense of themselves in relation to what they are learning. If the work is connected to their lived experiences in terms of their identities, locations, and learning styles, students become better aware of what they can achieve both individually and collectively. They gain confidence and experience excitement as they see creative spaces — these motivating classrooms — as places of possibility to develop a new kind of self.

Students often enter the classroom thinking that they are one kind of person. They think that their identity is fixed. By becoming involved in identity-forming exercises, students begin to see that there are many ways of communicating, many ways of being, many ways of responding, and many ways of thinking and representing. As they find creative ways to represent who they are and what they know, students begin to have a heightened sense of what they can achieve individually and with their peers. They learn to rely on others as they create meaning together. As a result, they become more generous with others, more forgiving, more open to difference, and less fearful of diverse viewpoints.

Some might say that these kinds of activities take up too much time and are not connected to the curriculum. My argument is that respect, reciprocity, and relationships have become the 3 Rs of education. Students need to acknowledge who is in the room, learn to be generous with one another, and understand that part of the work that lies ahead is to learn how to work together so that everyone can succeed academically and socially.

All students enter the classroom wanting to be accepted and needing to succeed academically. They *will* feel accepted and succeed in their studies if they believe that they have an opportunity to share the stories about where they are from so that they can get to where they are going.

3

Bringing the World into the Classroom — Inquiry

"A prudent question is one-half wisdom."
— Francis Bacon

An inquiry-based classroom is a place where both students and teachers ask authentic questions that provoke new understandings about the curriculum. The nature of such a classroom tends to be improvisational and have a certain kind of openness as students choose aspects of the curriculum that interest them, decide what they want to know, develop rich questions, devise a research plan, and then find a way of sharing their findings with others. The teacher's role in an inquiry-based classroom is to spark interest in the material, set out an array of learning opportunities, help students find a focus, and then encourage them to develop robust questions that guide their learning. Often, this kind of work allows students to enter into realms of learning not at first imagined.

Into New Realms of Learning

Inquiry-based classrooms are grounded in the students' curiosity about the curriculum at hand. Through inquiry, students can explore real and imagined worlds. For instance, they can work in math, science, and social science, discovering aspects to topics and ideas that are very complex. They can also work in the arts and humanities, allowing their imaginations to invent questions that provoke new understandings about various perspectives, personalities, relationships, events, and ways of knowing.

Inquiry-based classrooms are places that connect students' lived experiences to what the students need and want to learn. There is both individual and shared inquiry. Students might begin with a question of their own, listen to the questions of their peers, and then consolidate what they want to know in a more formal way.

Because questions beget questions, only a certain amount of planning can occur. As a result, teachers need to be open to the way in which the students respond to and interact with what they are finding out. They need to be prepared to change direction and follow along as students ask questions that take the inquiry into realms of learning that produce new discoveries and understandings.

When I work with students, I find out who they are, what they know, what they want to investigate, and why they want to know this. I then try very hard to set a larger context that allows everyone to see the interweaving of themes, topics, ideas, relationships, and concepts. We often expand the topic they have chosen so that more curriculum connections can be made.

Of course, if you are teaching just science, then by all means, call your unit "Erosion." It's when you are teaching an integrated unit, where you are combining subjects such as English, history, science, drama, art, and media studies, that you might need to expand the title.

Strategic title choice

The words used as a title for an inquiry project need to be chosen carefully. For instance, instead of simply calling an inquiry project "Erosion," perhaps it could be named "Disappearance." Consider which title has more potential for inquiry and imagination. Which word opens us up to more humanistic dimensions, more drama, more wonder, more story? *Erosion* seems to restrict us in some ways: it allows us to think only about the natural world in a scientific way. *Disappearance*, however, seems to be able to combine many worlds into one. We can look at the disappearance of physical things such as land and water, but we can also wonder about how the disappearance of life-giving forces can put pressures on human relationships and well-being so that other kinds of things — perhaps love and compassion, relationships, economic security, and home — go, too. To define an inquiry through its title becomes a way of identifying an overarching theme.

Collaborative inquiry design

As envisioned here, the inquiry process is collaborative. Teachers often work jointly to support one another as they design the beginnings of inquiry projects. They come together to examine their own educational practice and to encourage each other to teach in new ways. Teachers in inquiry-based classrooms need to be flexible people who want to collaborate with others, imagine together, engage in problem solving, and think about teaching in critical and creative ways. As they plan and then implement the projects, they are constantly analyzing, assessing, and evaluating what is working and what needs to be tweaked. They acknowledge that nothing is perfect, and they are comfortable thinking through the plan and then changing direction as soon as their students become engaged and in charge.

A Process Driven by Four Purposes

The inquiry process is driven by four purposes, each of which is discussed below:
- to increase student engagement
- to honor student voice
- to improve student achievement
- o allow teachers to develop and refine their teaching practice

Increasing student engagement

Inquiry-based classrooms are not quiet places. They are filled with conversation, action, and thinking. Students work in small groups, researching, planning, solving problems, creating, and representing their new understandings about material they care about. In my work, I notice that students pay attention, are curious, show interest, and persevere to find solutions to complex problems. A fair degree of happiness and optimism about the work are also apparent as the students move forward in their learning. They are motivated to keep going.

Towards Teaching in Conceptual Ways: Inquiry-based classrooms are associated with conceptual teaching but moving to that from procedural teaching is a challenge. In 2013, I was asked to participate in a research project on math and well-being in the Dufferin-Peel Catholic District School Board. I worked with the staff development, curriculum, and research teams to find connections between teaching math and empowering students to gain confidence in the learning process. It became clear that teachers needed to take risks in their teaching so that their students could learn in more open-ended ways. Teachers needed to give up the "right answer" approach and spend time helping students to play in the margins of understanding and to notice mathematical relationships. Teachers wanted to learn how to anticipate student response, to encourage thinking in math, and to plan accordingly. The overall goal was to help students see math in a whole different way and feel better about themselves as learners. I asked many questions as I helped ease teachers through the transition of teaching in procedural ways to teaching in conceptual ways.

I prompted the teachers to remember the last math lesson that they had taught, and then I asked the following questions:
- Did the task you assigned ask your students to follow instructions or solve problems?
- Did you encourage your students to invent other solutions and then tell you about their thinking?
- How do you see yourself as a math teacher?
- What is the experience of math in your classroom?

Dimensions of Student Engagement

In *What Did You Do in School Today?* J. Douglas Willms, Sharon Friesen, and Penny Milton (2009) identify three dimensions of student engagement:

- *social engagement:* A sense of belonging and participation in school life
- *academic or institutional engagement:* Participation in the formal requirements of schooling
- *intellectual engagement:* A serious emotional and cognitive investment in learning, using higher-order thinking skills (such as analysis and evaluation) to increase understanding, solve complex problems, or construct new knowledge

All four questions caused a certain amount of discomfort but led teachers into realms of discussion that moved them on in their practice.

Arresting Questions: In the Fall of 2013, I worked in a Grade 9 classroom with students who were about to read *Romeo and Juliet*. For many of them, it was their first experience reading a play by Shakespeare. We spent some time talking about how worried they were. Many said that their friends had told them that the language was too difficult.

I knew that I had to arrest their attention so I asked them two provocative questions: "What if a girl falls in love with a boy who has killed someone? What advice would you give her?"

The students became very emotional about these questions. They told personal stories of violence, loss, fear, betrayal, and the justice system. At the end of the discussion, I said: "Well, tomorrow when we begin to study *Romeo and Juliet*, you will meet two people who make very bad decisions in all sorts of ways. Juliet loves Romeo despite the fact that he has been involved in some very bad stuff. We will find out more tomorrow . . ."

What Underpins Student Engagement: So, student engagement relies a lot on the imaginations of teachers, and part of it has to do with creating questions and contexts to arrest the attention of students as they embark upon their learning journey.

Honoring student voice

I believe in creating an ethic of hearing every voice in the classroom. Sometimes, achieving this is difficult so there has to be a conscious effort to watch for those who are ignored or silenced or shunned for some reason. It also helps if teachers have an understanding of the importance of oral language: oral language encourages students' listening and observation skills, builds self-esteem and confidence, improves group work, develops trust and mutual appreciation, and enhances critical thought. Teachers need to be prepared to allow students to "talk themselves into understanding" as they work in partners, in small groups, or as a whole class. Inquiry-based projects promote accountable talk and purposeful discussion, and in my teaching, I have developed nine talk frames that help me guide the students into deeper levels of engagement and learning.

The talk frames are as follows: (1) social, (2) collaborative, (3) scaffolded, (4) interpretive, (5) modelled, (6) inclusive, (7) informed, (8) presentational, and (9) digital.

1. *Social Talk:* The need to explore one's growing understanding of self in relation to others is central to personal growth and social success as a contributing and productive individual and citizen. Informal discussion — or social talk, both on and off task — allows students to develop confidence and oral proficiency as they explore their social skills and their awareness of self and perspective on others. When we create climates for engaged conversations and genuine explorations through talk, we establish learning conditions that allow students to become more aware of themselves and others.

2. *Collaborative Talk:* Students explore their own and others' ideas about what they are learning. They learn how to listen intently and build on each other's ideas. If the work that students do together is challenging and intriguing, the talk that emanates from their experiences will be rich and rewarding. The art of collaboration is essential for problem solving and knowledge building.

    Students enjoy learning from and with their peers, and a large part of that learning centers on the way in which they talk with one another. Teachers need to give their students lots of time to talk to with one another in the classroom so that they can find out about one another, share ideas about what they are learning, reflect on new knowledge, gain new perspectives, analyze unforeseen problems, negotiate meaning, and talk themselves into understanding. By working jointly on a project or by solving a problem together, students gain more than just information. They begin to see other students as teachers as well — people whom they can spend time with to find out about what they need to know.

3. *Scaffolded Talk:* In classrooms where scaffolded talk occurs, the use of a variety of instructional strategies is evident. Teachers pay attention to the varying language facilities of their diverse students and work within that understanding. In other words, they listen for those students who hesitate and worry about their oral language function. Teachers include sentence stems or prompts, graphic organizers, structured groupings, and a wide variety of texts and media to encourage everyone to speak. When these strategies are in place, students have multiple opportunities to verbalize and articulate their thinking, in turn, developing conceptual understanding and creating new understanding and knowledge.

4. *Interpretive Talk:* Interpretive talk allows students to find ways to explore the meaning behind the words. It also gives them an opportunity to become aware of how language works. Problem-solving and inquiry skills are honed as students analyze and reflect on the various meanings in a text that were not apparent on a first reading. The work in the classroom should allow students to speak the words out loud *before* they fully understand them. In other words, engagement with texts often happens before comprehension. New understandings will be achieved as students work with texts in active and imaginative ways. If they have an opportunity to connect the texts to

their lived experiences, they will enjoy the journey towards interpretation that much more.

5. *Modelled Talk:* When adults in classrooms (teachers, artists, and other guests) talk powerfully and purposefully, they inspire students to listen. By choosing their words carefully, by presenting ideas powerfully, by reading with skill and an awareness of their audience as they talk, these adults give students an awareness of the power of the human voice. They also might encourage insights into how to present their own ideas in compelling ways.

6. *Inclusive Talk:* Though talking and learning together, students begin to feel connected to each other and to form "a community of learners" so that they can work through problems, ask questions for which there are many solutions, and enjoy learning with and from each other. Unless students feel emotionally and physically safe, they will not share personal thoughts and feelings, and discussions will be tinny, strained, and dishonest. This is why it is important to establish a sense of community in the classroom at the beginning of the year so that students will feel included and can begin to interact with and learn from each other.

    Inclusive classrooms put all learners in the forefront. Research tells us that in order for students to find their public voices to express who they are and what they are learning, they need to have a caring and empathetic teacher. They also require peer support — students in the classroom who cheer them on as they achieve small and large successes. A student's first language is valued and celebrated as a crucial part of his or her learning, and there is reciprocal respect among teachers and students. Listening to the silent voices is part of the teacher's ethical enterprise.

7. *Informed Talk:* Focused talk "informed" by ideas and insights that are gained through questioning, researching, exploring, and investigating helps all students become creative and critical thinkers. Informed talk also enables students to develop productive and engaged habits of mind and encourages them to take part in discussions that support learning. Classrooms that foster critical inquiry create contexts for students to express their emerging understanding and demonstrate their new knowledge. The skills of informed talk are developed when students are encouraged to consider new ideas or ways of thinking and consolidate their progress through exploration, research, and dialogue with peers and adults around compelling questions.

8. *Presentational Talk:* This kind of talk involves sharing, presenting, and performing. It is important for teachers to carefully scaffold the teaching of presentational skills so that they are building their students' self-esteem and confidence in speaking out loud to an audience. Students can move from sharing informally with a partner, to working as a group on a presentation where everyone says something, to full-fledged performing where the pressure to convey an idea powerfully is paramount.

9. *Digital Talk:* Digital talk allows students to be aware of the ways that language is conveyed through email, text messaging, and other forms, and how images and words can have a powerful effect on the reader or listener. Students can come to actively appreciate the effects of digital talk and the lack of nuance in abbreviated language use. As educators, we must help students develop the tools they need to sort, sift, and make personal sense of the information sources that surround their every inquiry. We need to help them be aware of their digital footprint, namely, that what is written or

---

One way to make presentational talk easier for some students is to encourage them to weave technology into their presentations. PowerPoints, YouTube videos, Prezi, and other kinds of visual aids can enhance a presentation and take the focus off the speaker for a little bit.

said on the Internet cannot be erased. We can also help them learn how to be critically aware of what they are reading and being exposed to.

> "A bird doesn't sing because it has an answer, it sings because it has a song."
> — Maya Angelou

Student voice is not just about speaking. It is also about thinking, interacting with others, and asking critical questions that encourage new understandings. There are multiple ways for students to ask questions — through writing and through the expressive arts — and the way in which they investigate material and then represent their understanding can take many forms, including dance, sculpture, painting, film, and theatre. No matter the medium, these are the questions that students and teachers can reflect on individually and collectively:

- How do I personally connect to this material?
- What does this [photo, article, character, discussion] remind me of?
- What more do I want to know about this?
- Why do I want to know this?
- Who might help me?
- What resources might I find out about?
- Who or what could help me find those resources?
- What are my strengths in a group situation?
- What group skills do I need to work on?
- What do we think we learned?
- What worked? What didn't?
- What might we do differently next time?

> "*Why* is in our DNA."
> — Billboard sign outside the Princess Margaret Cancer Centre, Toronto

These types of questions are instrumental to growth at all levels of learning.

Improving student achievement

Assessment and evaluation practices have encountered a paradigm shift. Previously, teachers designed the learning goals, delivered the instruction, and evaluated the student work. In current practice, the processes of assessment *for* learning and assessment *as* learning see teachers working collaboratively with students, sharing learning goals, co-constructing criteria, and sharing feedback. In this model, students are at the center of the assessment process, which is no longer an event or mystery.

The assessment *for* and *as* learning models work together to support students' learning. Students need to be able to explain their thinking to teachers and peers. When they can do so, it deepens their understanding of their learning processes and the content knowledge they are learning. In addition, when students share their thinking, teachers gain a deeper understanding of *what they will need to do next* to support and enhance student learning. Talking with students about what is important to their learning, as well as offering exemplars to review, helps students understand what successful achievement looks like.

In order to become independent learners and thinkers, students must develop self-assessment and goal-setting skills. Identifying and practicing these skills empower students to become responsible for their learning and to act on the next steps that will move them towards success. The ability to self-assess — to be metacognitive about one's thinking and learning — is empowering for students and a goal for learners. We are educating students for careers or roles that have not even been created. In order for them to be flexible thinkers able to meet the needs of these roles, it is essential that students develop metacognitive skills.

The Signs of Collegiality
Roland Barth (1990) reminds us that collegiality in schools is signaled by the presence of four behaviors:

1. Adults talk about practice. These conversations are frequent, continuous, concrete, and precise.
2. Adults observe each other engaged in teaching and administration.
3. Adults engage in work on curriculum by planning, designing, researching, and evaluating curriculum.
4. Adults reveal, articulate, and share with one another what they know about the art and craft of teaching.

Refining teacher practice

Given the structure of schools and the challenges of time, how can teachers do all this work? In my opinion, the work begins with the openness of the teacher to teach and assess in this way — to have the student at the center of the learning experience. Many teachers have told me that their inquiry-based classrooms are the "right fit" for them — for their teaching philosophy, for the kinds of students they teach, for the kinds of curriculum connections they want to make, and for the communities that they serve. The right fit is important. Teachers need to know that deep learning is achievable if they open up the curriculum to imaginative exploration: if they give students choice, permission, and support in the inquiry process. Teachers need to be able to listen, gauge interest, provide resources, improvise, and work alongside their students, asking significant questions and moving them along. One teacher I work with talks about "inching along" with her students as learning unfolds.

Most important, however, is the kind of support that teachers have from their principal and from their peers to imagine a classroom that is different: a classroom that hums with the kinds of rich and robust questions that keep people searching to know more but also to think and feel differently all at the same time. Collegiality among teachers and the administration plays a key part in the creation of a dynamic inquiry-based classroom.

Towards Collaborative Inquiry

Teaching teams — either divisional teams or teachers with a desire to work on a theme-based project — work together to develop the inquiry question. They gather and analyze evidence, determine next steps, and share their findings and recommendations. Finding the common ground among teachers is important. Time needs to be devoted to academic conversations about teaching and learning. Administrators need to be part of this to support the planning through release time and other means. Because collaborative inquiry is driven by students' learning needs and interests, the context of each classroom and the location and identities of the students need to be taken into account.

Criteria for a good inquiry question

Examples of Well-Rounded Inquiry Questions
Primary: If bees became extinct, how would farmers and food production all over the world be affected?
Junior: In what ways does opening a mine both help and harm a community?
Intermediate: How do I keep my digital footprint safe on the Internet?

Here are four criteria based on notes by Catherine Schmidt-Jones for developing a good inquiry question.

1. Is it challenging? If the learner can simply look up the answer and easily understand it, a structured inquiry is not needed.
2. Is it within reach of the learner? If the learner will not likely make much progress in answering the question even after several weeks of reasonable effort, adopting a different, more manageable question would be wise.
3. Will it lead the learner to new understanding, skills, and ways of thinking? Remember that concentrating on the learning of new "facts" is *not* the best goal.
4. Is it of intrinsic interest to the learner? A teacher may provide suggestions and guidance, may even insist that the inquiry take a certain form or lead towards a particular skill or type of understanding, but the question should be one that the learner wants to answer.

Planning as a tentative endeavor

A certain messiness is associated with the inquiry approach. Much of the initial work is tentative because the teachers can plan only so far. They need to meet with their students and discover what the students want to know. In the initial planning sessions, one teacher in the *All I's on Education* project said: "We can't go much further in our planning. We have a map, but now it is up to the students to take us down the curriculum path. This is both scary and exciting, and I hope that I am up for all this!"

Seven steps to fulfilling an inquiry project

1. The students are presented with the topic, which is drawn from provincial or state expectations.
2. Through various activities, the teacher finds out what the students already know about the topic and helps them generate questions to explore.
3. The questions that students formulate are recorded, analyzed, rated, and ranked. These questions point the students in the direction of resources that will help them make their inquiry.
4. Students begin their research by developing a plan of where to retrieve information. The Internet is an obvious choice, but they may also be able to interview people in the community, Skype with an author, or invite a scientist or an artist into the classroom. Perhaps they could go on a field trip or a community walk, taking research materials such as cameras, iPads, and sketchbooks with them. Books, articles, newspapers, magazines, blogs, and emails all provide other research venues.
5. Students informally share their initial discoveries and understandings with the rest of the class. The way in which students share information needs to be structured and rehearsed.
6. Students share their work with others in a culminating activity — this is a much more formal stage in the process.
7. The results of the student inquiry are reviewed and evaluated by the class, the teacher, and others.

See "Ways to Share Initial Findings and Present New Understandings," starting on page 67. The line master on page 70, "How to Support Research," can be used as a planning aid by students in their small groups.

How Inquiry Projects Benefit Students

Setting up inquiry projects in classrooms can be challenging, but such projects provide a way to acknowledge the diversity of learners and to keep students engaged with learning. Because the students identify what and how they want to learn, an inquiry project is a perfect way for students to individually and collectively construct new knowledge of something they care about. Inquiry projects build awareness of the world beyond the classroom and beyond the students' textbooks. They also build community in the classroom as students rely upon one another to create questions, research, and present new ideas.

Kinds of Questions for an Inquiry-Based Classroom

As the second and third steps in establishing an inquiry-based classroom indicate, student-generated questions are vital to the process. The purpose of student-generated questions is to help students think more deeply and critically about something that fascinates them. These initial questions allow students to use their imaginations to think about questions that are important to ask, even if there are conflicting answers, multiple answers, or no answers.

In his article "The Long Trip," William Ayers, for one, encourages students "to develop an authentic question about the world, a question of some urgency or personal meaning, and then to go out and find the answer to that question by getting close to it, by touching it, and to document the whole process in a variety of ways" (1988, 95). I am always moved by these words, especially the part about having students *touch* a question — to find personal meaning, to be engaged with stuff that matters in their lives. Ideally, all the questions students formulate for an inquiry will provoke them and demand to be addressed.

So, how do teachers encourage students to ask questions that matter . . . that lead them into new realms of understanding? I have identified four kinds of questions that can be used in an inquiry-based classroom: (1) questions that draw on what students already know and remember; (2) questions that allow students to imagine forward and be open to multiple answers, not worrying unduly about right answers; (3) questions that allow students to synthesize their thoughts and opinions; and (4) questions that enable students to make judgments and decisions and ultimately defend them. No progression is intended to the order of these kinds of questions, and they often get jumbled as classroom discussions enter different realms.

The chart below identifies these four kinds of questions and provides appropriate question prompts. Note that, even though a given question can be answered by a simple yes or no, from experience, I find that it still serves as an initial prompt into something calling for more detail.

FOUR KINDS OF QUESTIONS

Questions that draw upon what students already know:	**Questions that allow students to imagine multiple answers:**	**Questions that allow students to synthesize information:**	**Questions that prompt students to make evaluations or judgments:**
Examples: Do you recall . . . ? Remember when . . . ? Do you recognize . . . ? What happened . . . ? Do we know enough to begin?	*Examples:* What would happen if . . . ? Do you suppose . . . ? I wonder how . . . ? What might have happened if . . . ? Why would they have made that decision? What better ways can we think of? What might happen when . . . ? I wonder what would make a person . . . ?	*Examples:* Is it possible? Should we assume therefore that . . . ? How do we know . . . ? How does this new information fit with what we already know? What is the difference . . . ? Why is this . . . ?	*Examples:* Which is better? Why is this false? Could this be true? How would this play out if . . . ? What's the best way to . . . ?

Developing Rich Questions: Six Approaches

The Ability to Discern

"An education isn't how much you have committed to memory, or even how much you know. It's being able to differentiate between what you do know and what you don't."
— Anatole France

Initial Questions
- What do we know?
- What do we want to know?
- Who could answer some of these questions?

Developing rich questions for inquiry takes practice. Here are some well-tested approaches whereby students can gain practice asking questions that will lead to new understandings.

Approach 1: From Question to Question

I ask students to form five groups, hand out two large pieces of chart paper and markers to each group, and prompt them to appoint a recorder. I read aloud to the class the following newspaper snippet (created out of my imagination) twice.

> Five school children found a baby on a commuter train between Toronto and Newmarket. The baby was wrapped in a pink woollen blanket and was found in the train's washroom. Authorities were notified. The baby is now in the care of the Children's Aid Society until its parent or guardian can be found.

I give a newspaper date and then ask the recorders to put the following title at the top of the first piece of chart paper: *What do we know?*

I give each group a copy of the text just read aloud. The students then read the snippet to extract "just the facts" and list them. As a class, we list all the key details that each group has generated. Here is what one class came up with:

> This event happened 18 years ago.
> A baby was found by 5 school children on a commuter train in the train's washroom.
> The train was travelling between Toronto and Newmarket.
> The baby was wrapped in a pink woollen blanket.
> Authorities were called.
> The baby was put in the care of the Children's Aid Society.

Once we have shared "just the facts," I ask the recorders to turn the sheet over and write the following title at the top of the sheet: *What do we want to know?*

The students are encouraged to go beyond merely factual wonderings to questions that will make them think about this incident in deeper, more insightful ways.

My goal is to move students on from initial questions like these: Was the baby a boy or a girl? How old were the schoolchildren? Why were they on the train? Was there a teacher present? What time of day was it? What did the students do immediately after they found the baby? Who called the authorities? What happened after the police were called?

Instead, I want the students to pose questions that involve more critical thinking and imaginative response. Was the baby crying when the students discovered it? How did the baby end up in the washroom? Was it in a sink? on the floor? on a stall? Did the baby appear to be sick? Was it wearing anything under the blanket? Was the diaper clean or dirty? Was anyone in the washroom when they discovered the baby? How long had the baby been in the washroom? Was a note left with the baby? If so, what did it say? Was there a diaper bag left with the baby? If so, what was in it? How did the baby respond to being found?

57

I then ask the recorders to write the following at the top of another sheet: *Who could answer some of these questions?* In small groups, the students brainstorm a list of people, coming up with ideas like these: one of the school children, the supervising teacher, the train conductor, the police, a Children's Aid Society worker, a passenger on the train, the person who cleans the train, a commuter.

I ask for five volunteers and invite them to look at the list of possible people to question. They each decide on a role to adopt. They are not allowed to confer with one another. They stand quietly and alone in five different locations in the classroom.

I then set the context, saying: "It is now 18 years since the baby was abandoned on the train outside of Toronto. The baby has grown up to be a successful graduate of a high school but is keen to find out what happened on that day. A group of people who were witnesses to the event long ago have agreed to come together to answer some questions so that this young person can get some insight into what happened. The community of friends have gathered to ask questions to see if they can piece the story together at last."

The five groups of students now use the template "Four Kinds of Questions" to develop questions related to a specific character. Here are a few representative examples:

- For the supervising teacher — recalling
  Do you recall how many students you were supervising on that day, and how the baby's situation was revealed to you?
- For the CAS worker — imagining
  What might have happened if the baby had not been discovered when it was?
- For the police officer — synthesizing
  Is it possible that the person who was looking after the baby was in some kind of distress and only left the baby for a few minutes?
- For one of the school children — evaluating
  How has this event that happened a long time ago affected your life?

The volunteer students sit on chairs in either a full or half circle (I prefer full) and answer questions from the members of the community sitting on chairs in a larger circle. As teacher I facilitate the questioning and the story unfolds.

At the conclusion of the exercise, these questions *about* the questions might be asked of the students:

- What were the most powerful questions?
- Why? What made them powerful?
- What kinds of information do questions like these generate?
- How do you make sure that you ask questions that make you think?

Approach 2: Hot Seating

Hot seating is an activity where the students, as themselves, have the opportunity to question or interview a role player who remains in character. The role player sits in the "hot seat" as a character from the play or story either at the front of the classroom or in a small group and answers questions from the students. I often help students think about the kinds of questions they want to ask and use the template "Four Kinds of Questions," shown above.

I employ this teaching strategy when I work with plays, novels, and historical incidents, where students can hot-seat historical characters. For example, assume that it is 1534 and explorer Jacques Cartier is recruiting sailors for his ships to the New World. In role as the recruitment officer, you could interview and hire sailors to make the journey. Criteria for successful selection would include a willingness to take orders, a sense of adventure, and an ability to withstand long days and hours of cold and hunger. A hot-seated person — in this case, a candidate for sailor — should be a volunteer who likes the challenge of answering questions spontaneously. The questions you ask of the person will allow you to deepen student commitment, assess prior knowledge, challenge students to think creatively, and create a base of knowledge from which the class can work.

Before you hot-seat any applicants, though, have the students fill out application forms that will serve as the basis of questions asked aloud and give "hot-seaters" a head start on how to respond. Small groups or the whole class can work together to frame at least five questions.

Students can take turns sitting in the hot seat as the same character, or they can assume new characters. They can even invent characters not in the play or story, but plausible to the plot.

The purpose of hot seating is to open up the story for reflection and debate. Students improvise answers to questions, and both "hot-seaters" and questioners can wonder aloud about characters, relationships, incidents, feelings, actions, and consequences. If working in small groups, students can later share inventive questions and answers in whole-class discussion.

Here are three sets of hot-seating questions raised by students.

Romeo and Juliet: Hot-Seating the Nurse
What was Juliet like as a little girl?
Do you think she loved you more than she loved her mother?
What kind of hold did Juliet have on your emotions?
Why did you take the chances that you did?
Did you have Juliet's best interests at heart when you allowed her to meet with Romeo?
Since Juliet's death, what is your relationship with Juliet's parents?
Have you sought forgiveness from them?
If so, how did they react?
If you are fired because of what you did, where will you go?
Tell us about the nightmares you have been experiencing since Juliet's death.
If you could change just one thing that you did, what would it be?

Hamlet: Hot-Seating the Ghost of Hamlet's Father
Is it correct that there were no witnesses to the murder?
What memories do you have of the incident?
What would have happened if the murder had not been successful?
What kinds of revenge would you have sought for your wife and Claudius?
How would you describe your relationship to your son, Hamlet?
How would you describe your marriage to Gertrude?
What was your reaction when you discovered that your wife married your brother so soon after your death?
How do you feel about that?
What insights can you offer into the soul of Claudius?

Before all this happened, what was the mental and physical condition of your son?
Did your son show signs of indecision and unhappiness, or did this all come about after your death?
I am sure that you have thought about ways you can help Hamlet from the other side. Please describe them.
What can you tell us about the afterlife in general?

Macbeth: **Hot-Seating Lady Macbeth's Maid (an invented character)**
How long have you worked for the Macbeths?
How would you rate them as employers?
When you were asked to clean up the blood in King Duncan's chamber, what was your reaction, and then, what were your thoughts?
How did you react when you were asked to keep this whole thing a secret?
When you eavesdrop on the Macbeths' conversations late at night, what do you hear them saying?
What kinds of conclusions are you drawing from what you have seen and heard?

Approach 3: The Expert Game

The Expert Game helps students generate questions in small groups as they conduct an interview in role. It provides students with authentic, although imagined contexts that require them to ask questions, listen, synthesize information, infer, and make a judgment. Here is how to play it.

"Number yourselves off from 1 to 5. Number 1 is going to be an expert. In this case, number 1 is going to be an underwater diver who is an expert at finding ancient treasures. The rest of you (2, 3, 4, and 5) are the owners of the International Treasure Hunt Company. You require the expertise of an underwater diver to make a series of dangerous, but lucrative discoveries.

"I want to speak to the experts privately. In the meantime, members of each interviewing team need to determine what qualities and expertise you would like this underwater diver to have and to come up with some introductory questions. Remember to make this a formal interview and to set up the scene so that all of you will be facing the interviewee."

In a private conversation, tell the experts that they are to pretend to know as much as they can about underwater diving. Encourage them to use their imaginations and to be as serious as possible about this role. Send the experts back to their groups, and then say:

"On my signal, I want you to begin the interview. Invite the candidate to sit down and then begin the questioning."

The interviews last three or four minutes. Once they are finished, ask one interviewer per group to stand; then, pose a few questions such as the following:

"At this point in the interview, what is your overall impression of the candidate? Are you leaning towards hiring him [or her]? Why or why not?

What further questions would you like to ask before you make your decision?"

After the practice session, make sure that everyone in the group has a chance to play an expert. Other recommended expert roles include an expert detective, an expert athletic coach, an expert concert organizer, an expert teen magazine editor, and an expert body piercer.

Answering as Experts
I once worked with a Grade 9 class that had read an article about the pros and cons of body piercing. After their reading, we played the Expert Game in small groups. The student volunteers showed that they had understood the article through their ability to answer the questions posed by the hiring committee of health officials. The teacher and I were able to assess the students' reading comprehension of the article by listening to the way in which the students incorporated what they had read into the role-playing situations.

Approach 4: Teacher in Role

Sometimes, the teacher works in role and the students, also in role, interview to obtain information. The teacher in role is able to work inside the situation, creating a climate where the honesty of individual contributions is valued and respect is shown to everyone who contributes ideas. The teacher in role imbues the situation with seriousness of purpose and adds an element of tension to the work in role. I call this "teaching for tension." Teacher in role allows a teacher to move from the teacher stance of "one who knows all" to "someone who needs to know more."

Teacher in role is also a wonderful way to model questioning and searching for answers. When I work this way I am careful to prepare what I am going to say in my introductory remarks. I keep in mind that I must give a clear definition of *who* I am, *where* I am, and *what* is happening so that the class begins to understand the context and figure out who *they* are in the drama. I take my time and do not give too much information away too early. In this way, I am introducing nuance and subtlety, enticing the students into the story — leading them on, intriguing them so that they will want to know more.

I have used this technique hundreds of times in classrooms as I introduce themes, novels, and historical events. What appeals to students and surprises them is that the teacher is willing to shift the classroom dynamic and to give over power to the students for a period of time. The role-playing unlocks new avenues of understanding and allows students to relate to the characters they are meeting with an immediacy both enjoyable and memorable. It also lets students have an opportunity to practice different language registers as they speak as adults who have some authority or experience.

STUDENTS PROBE FOR CLUES WITH PURPOSE

I worked with a teacher in an English Language Learner (ELL) classroom where the students were newly arrived to the country and had little English language skill. We decided to initiate a drama in which the teacher would introduce a woman whom she had found on her porch that morning. The woman appeared to be disoriented and refused to speak, although it was obvious she could understand.

The class had to find ways of getting the woman to tell her story. They became a hospital staff and set up a reception area as well as a waiting room for other visitors. They adopted roles as an interview team: student doctors who were learning how to interview patients who had been traumatized in some way. They created lists of questions.

As teacher in role, I played the disoriented person. The students wanted to see if I had anything in my purse that might give them clues as to who I was. I had keys, a picture of a baby, and a note in English written in difficult script and with challenging words: "If you encounter this person and she appears disoriented, keep her safe, phone this number and talk to whomever answers the phone. This person has a medical condition that makes her extremely anxious. She is not dangerous and likes tea with biscuits."

It was remarkable to watch these ELL students strive to speak to get the "lady on the porch" to tell her story. They persevered in their questions and found out what they could.

ALTERNATIVE TEACHER-IN-ROLE SCENARIOS

Here are a few other scenarios where teachers can adopt a role. I have provided opening lines.

As the mayor of a town looking for a new site for a dump:

> I know that a lot of you have come to this meeting wanting to stop this whole enterprise, but we really don't have very many options. We need to find a way to take care of our garbage. We are a community that is growing very quickly. Unless we can think of something new, I am afraid that we will have to go with the original plan. I am here to listen to your concerns and to give you time to devise a new solution, if there is one.

As the general manager of a mine that has collapsed with miners in grave danger below, meeting with a team of rescuers:

> If we do decide to use dynamite in the mine shaft, we run the risk of total mine collapse. Is there another option, do you think, to bring the men to safety?

As a medical officer of health during a pandemic appealing to the community to work together:

> We need to make a list of rules to live by so that we all do not become infected. What are some of your suggestions given the severity of the problem?

Approach 5: Students in Professional Roles Asking Questions

Questioning can be integrated into the planning of an inquiry, including that for a cross-grade integrated science, visual arts, and drama unit, as I describe below.

As part of the *All I's on Education* project, I worked with three teachers and students in French at L'école élémentaire LaFontaine on an intense inquiry project about the impact that fracking, or drilling and injecting fluid into the ground at a high pressure in order to fracture shale rocks to release natural gas inside, was having on the ecosystem. We decided that the Grade 4/5 students would become scientists researching the impact of fracking on the ecosystem. These Junior students would present their research to the Grade 1 students involved with the project, explaining the environmental problems associated with fracking. They would then enlist the help of the younger students as "inventors," and the inventors would develop solutions to the challenges. Having both groups of students in role provided the Grade 4/5 students with an opportunity to work from a position of power.

In an email to the teachers, I explained how questioning promotes understanding for all the students in role and for the teachers. I wrote:

"The role of educated, professional scientists allows students to conduct their research with a seriousness of purpose. I would like to suggest that you spend some time having them 'get into role.' Perhaps each scientist could have a name (e.g., Dr. Renée Leblanc) as well as a certain expertise in the global scientific community. ('I have won many awards because of my research on the disappearance of frogs and toads because of the change in the ecosystem.')

"I have provided a series of questions that you might use to deepen the students' understanding of their scientist role:

> You are a world-renowned scientist who has been invited to investigate the impact of mineral extraction on the environment. Before you begin your research with your colleagues, we would like you to fill out the following form:
>
> - What is your name?
> - What universities did you attend?
> - When did you graduate?
> - Why did you decide to become a scientist?
> - In your opinion, how are scientists important to the future of the planet?
> - What is your greatest concern about the current state of the environment?
> - Why do you hold that opinion?

Not only will these questions help the students get into role, they will also allow you to diagnostically assess what the students already know and what they want to know."

As part of the exercise, the Grade 1 students were each provided with "An Inventor Kit," comprised of inventor glasses, a sketchbook, and a special colored pencil that would allow them to sketch and write about their ideas as they thought about them. The way that the teachers would know that the Grade 1 students were in inventing mode was when the students donned their inventor glasses. The culminating task took place when the Grade 1 students in role as inventors presented the Grade 4/5 students in role as scientists with their innovative ideas.

Approach 6: The 5 Ws

Many teachers use the 5 Ws approach as a way into inquiry. I like this frame a lot, but I also like to "mix and match the 5 Ws" so that questions flow in an easier manner. Students can explore all sorts of ideas and concepts if they push themselves beyond easier questions into more difficult and open-ended ones. Working in small groups, they appoint a recorder and a spokesperson so that they can share ideas with the rest of the class. For instance, they can explore literary texts or historical material by asking questions that draw on the 5 Ws — who, where, when, what, and why. Once they have worked together in small groups on one of the Ws, they come up with a question for the class.

Who? Who are the characters? What is their relationship to one another? What is interesting about them? What makes them "tick"? Is there a conflict between them? How do you envision them speaking? Given the description in the novel, how do you imagine that they look? What costume pieces can you imagine they would wear? Would you like to know them? If you met them on the street, what questions would you ask them? Who do they remind you of in your personal life, in your literary life, in your film life?

Where? Where is the setting? Where and how are the characters speaking? What do you imagine the setting to be like? If you were asked to create a film set for a scene in part of the novel, what would it look like? How would the characters use the space that you have imagined? How would they move around in the space? What kinds of props would you make? How would the characters use these props?

When? When is the story set? What do you know about this time period? What kinds of things were going on at this time? How would those events affect the action or characters?

What? What is happening in this scene? What are the characters doing? Why are they doing it?

Why? Why do the characters talk and act as they do? If you were in their predicament, what would you do?

Below is an illustration of the approach based on *The Boy on the Porch* by Sharon Creech. After students in a Grade 4 class had read the first four chapters of the book, they worked in small groups, each group exploring one of the 5 Ws. Here are some of their responses:

Group 1: Who?
We imagine the man in the book to be wearing worn overalls or jeans with a checked shirt. The overalls would have some dirt on them (from milking the cows in the barn), but the shirt would appear very clean (and ironed). The woman would be wearing a dress that is worn at the edges. The little boy would be in ripped clothes that look like hand-me-downs. We imagine that the couple had always wanted children but never had any. They would be nervous and excited to have found the boy on the porch. This is our *Who* question for the class: Who are the boys' parents?

Group 2: Where?
We imagine the house to be pretty run-down and the porch to have bits of broken-down furniture on it. The house is at the end of a long road and the barn is quite far from the house. There are no neighbors for many miles so the 3 characters are pretty isolated. We also think that there needs to be a screen door that squeaks when it opens and closes. The kitchen looks poor but is very clean. This is our *Where* question for the class: How would the boy have been left there without the man and the woman hearing people doing that?

Group 3: When?
We think that this story must have happened a long time ago because the story just has that kind of feel to it. We imagine that the man and the woman have an old car that sits in the driveway. We don't think that there is a phone in the house. We are not sure of the time period. Here is our *When* question for the class: At what time of the day was the boy left on the porch?

Group 4: What?
The man and the woman appear to be really nervous and excited. The man is very emotional but hides his feelings. We think that the man and the woman always wanted a child and now is their chance. The little boy might be too afraid to talk or maybe he can't. He does not seem afraid of the man and the woman. He reaches into his pocket to

pull out the note so he must know why he has been left there. Here is our *What* question for the class: What are the man and the woman going to do now that they have the note?

Group 5: Why?
The man and the woman seem really nervous. They don't really understand what happened to the boy and they are worried that he isn't speaking to them. Maybe they are afraid that they will be accused of stealing the child. They need to get in touch with the police before that happens. That's what we would do if this happened to us. Here is our *Why* question for the class: Why would parents give up their child to strangers even for just a little while?

How to Support Students in Fulfilling Their Research Tasks

> **The Need for Authentic Relationships**
>
> "Every human being is driven to search for meaning. We all try to create patterns from our environment and we all learn to some extent through interaction with others. Because ours is a social brain, it's important to build authentic relationships in the classroom and beyond."
> — Geoffrey Caine and Renate N. Caine, *Making Connections: Teaching and the Human Brain*, page 4

Students can work independently or in small groups on their inquiry projects, but groups have the greatest potential. Biologists have learned that the most powerful survival principle of life is diversity: there is no single right way that works — there will be hundreds or thousands of ways (Suzuki 1997, 7). In keeping with that understanding, we ask students to work in groups because we believe that a variety of ideas pooled together produces a better product. Students can reach goals that could not be attained efficiently by working independently. This belief holds true if negotiation is part of the process and if everyone has a voice in what happens in the group. Ensuring these things means that competition must be diminished and collaboration established and nurtured. For a classroom environment in which every student feels respected and has responsibility within a group, there needs to be acceptance of the importance of teamwork.

The importance of teaching group process skills

Figuring out group constellations — in other words, who is going to work with whom — is critical. Teachers will need groups of students who can work well together and can share the group tasks and the maintenance functions.

The problem is that typically we ask students to work in groups, but we do not teach them how to do so. By the time students reach Grade 3 or 4, they have had both good and bad experiences of working in groups. They are aware that group work can be fraught with competition, domination, exclusion, and unfairness. Some students, imagining that they will be forced out or dominated by other group members, shut down before they begin. Others remain determined to work only with those students whom they know are responsible and can be counted on to do their share of the work. Sometimes, a group goal is achieved by only a few of the members, and much disappointment and resentment will linger in the classroom. Goals are achieved, but often the group breaks apart in the process. Sometimes, the group fails to achieve anything at all.

Just as students need to be equipped with information about how to become effective readers and writers, they need to be taught group process skills so that they can achieve together rather than separately. Students need to become aware of how groups function, the different ways that a group can reach a decision, what kinds of behavior people manifest in group situations, and what other roles and responsibilities they might consider to make the groups that they find themselves in function better.

There are many ways to teach about group interaction. The trick is to make it simple so that students enjoy learning about it. This kind of learning is invaluable for them. They will use these skills and information throughout their lives both in school and beyond. They will also begin to be aware of how important it is to share the influence in a group and experience the satisfaction that comes from everyone being a part of a successfully completed task.

"Group decision-making is one of the most significant aspects of group functioning," write Johnson and Johnson (2014, 62). Students need to be taught that the best way to work in groups is to strive to reach a consensus so that most members can live with the decisions made. Often, students average the opinions or take a vote. That can be a way of making the decisions quickly, but it often is not a way to make everyone feel that they have a stake in what is being done. To reach consensus everyone must be able to voice an opinion and be heard. Everyone also must be willing to let go of some of what they want in order for a decision to be made.

Promoting positive group interactions

Your role as teacher is to constantly check in and find out how things are going. You are interested in the task, but you are also interested in how students are functioning as group members. Essentially, a group must do two things:
- achieve its goal — a task of some significance
- support itself so that the working relationships among the group members do not falter and all agreed-upon tasks are carried out

Because of this, at the end of each working session I ask my students these three questions:

1. Is the group getting closer to achieving its goal?
2. Is the group maintaining itself so that everyone feels that they are a contributing and valued member?
3. What are people doing that is making these two things happen?

Sometimes, I ask each group member to fill out a sheet based on the following statements, each of which identifies appropriate group behavior:

> We are clear about the task.
> We have agreed to work together.
> We are listening to each other.
> We are trying not to interrupt each other.
> We are including everyone in the discussion.
> We are making sure that we stay on task.
> We are taking short breaks when we need them.
> We are dividing up the work.
> We are following through.
> We are working from our strengths.
> We are monitoring the process.
> We are teaching each other about what we know.

We have agreed on the roles and responsibilities of each group member for this assignment.
We are determined to finish the task and remain a coherent group.

Defining group roles and responsibilities

Students need time to get to know one another's strengths. For example, one person may have an aptitude for graphs and numbers, another may be very good at addressing details, and another may have excellent oral presentation skills. They can adopt various roles as researchers:

- **visioners:** These people have a vision for the overall project as well as the energy, commitment, and sensitivity to get everyone on board. They are able to categorize ideas and are adept at making mind maps and other visual aids to keep the group motivated and interested. They do not dominate but have the end in sight and can help people move towards that goal. They encourage everyone to see the road ahead and keep the vision alive.
- **information gatherers:** These people have access to information on their tablets or the time to do the research, process it, and bring back information for the group to mull over. They are the foragers of information, and they lay what they have gleaned out for the group to digest. Their research skills are crucial to the success of the project.
- **technicians:** These people can make the technology work. They know the apps that can be downloaded, have the technical knowledge to record the conversations that are happening and are able to enhance the final presentation. They make everyone look good in the final presentation and support everyone in the process.
- **curators:** These people help create and then choose a series of artifacts that represent the inquiry project in precise, memorable, and artistic ways. They manage what has been produced in the inquiry and oversee the care of these items. They help in staging any exhibition of what has been learned and also help develop the project with the end in mind. Their artistic sensibilities give the group a real sense of achievement.
- **organizers:** These people have the ability to set schedules, organize data, keep the group focused, and remind group members about meetings and expectations. As process-oriented producers, they make the whole inquiry hum with a certain amount of dedicated intensity.

These roles need not be rigidly assigned, but everyone in a group should have a chance to explore each role at least for a day or two.

As the inquiry question is refined and explored, the ideas will have to be organized and shaped, a process that takes time and possibly experimentation. It is probably best to give students an informal opportunity to present their findings to the class before the culminating event. Such opportunities are described below.

Ways to Share Initial Findings and Present New Understandings

At the halfway mark, plan to give the groups an opportunity to informally share their inquiry projects so that everyone stays engaged and is aware of what else needs to be done. You could have each group appoint a spokesperson. This

---

I like to have students "practice" group process during group assignments. I choose two people to work together, and I have them observe the group and give feedback to group members. The students I choose must be diplomatic and sensitive; they must also realize the importance of being positive and encouraging.

"Rubric: CLEAR Criteria" is an assessment tool that groups can use as they hear the oral presentations of their peers. See page 69.

Speaking Well
"Talking and eloquence are not the same: to speak and to speak well are two things. A fool may talk but a wise man speaks."
— Ben Jonson

person will summarize the essence of the inquiry project (to date) and then present these ideas to the rest of the class. But the spokesperson does not do all the preparation. In order for spokespersons to speak with confidence to the audience, members of their groups need to ensure that they understand the topic and can summarize the main points discussed. That means each member can expect to articulate for the group what he or she has discovered and learned.

The group members become the spokesperson's supporters by helping their designate prepare what to say and how to say it publicly. They encourage the spokesperson to "have a go" and then listen for ways to improve the presentation. Be sure to remind the students that group members should be kind to one another and help students who are learning English or who fear public speaking to gain courage to speak publicly.

Another useful way to differentiate presentation tasks is for each student to handle a different aspect:

Student 1: The beginning
Student 2: What we plan to discuss
Student 3: Our chosen focus
Student 4: Our examples
Student 5: The ending

In this way, the group members become presenters as well as directors, stage managers, and producers. Everyone's presentation matters, and all students should experience feeling supported.

Many researchers of creativity often express that nothing of lasting value is understood in isolation. In Chapter 4, I will identify how to explore various disciplines in lasting ways — to have students inquire, analyze, interpret, create, represent, and present. Critical and integrative thinking often go hand in hand. Boundless inquiry is sometimes hard to achieve and can happen only if students are taught how to ask open-ended questions about material that matters. In the end, the important thing for teachers to do is to lay out something of worth to learn, give students choice about how to proceed, and then encourage them to ask critical questions that lead them into new realms of understanding.

Rubric: CLEAR Criteria

This rubric applies to oral presentations of inquiry projects in progress.

C is for Clarity.

3 The purpose is clear and captures the audience's attention. The vocabulary is descriptive and accurate, engaging the listener through imagery.
2 The purpose is apparent and the audience is listening. The vocabulary provides clarity and avoids confusion.
1 The purpose is not evident, and the audience is not engaged. The vocabulary is awkward or inappropriate for the topic, making the speaker difficult to understand.

L is for Learning.

3 The presenter has chosen appropriate language, compelling examples, and inventive technology that all work together to heighten the audience's interest and connection to the topic.
2 The presenter has taken some risks to keep the audience attentive and engaged.
1 The presenter is able to convey basic information so that the audience learns something new.

E is for Effective.

3 The content is organized logically, the transitions are fluid, and the audience stays focused throughout the entire presentation.
2 The organization of the content is congruent, transitions are evident, and the audience is usually focused throughout the presentation.
1 The content lacks organization, transitions are abrupt and distracting, and the audience is disengaged from the presentation.

A is for Authentic.

3 The presenter has included relevant details to add interest, depth, and authenticity to the presentation, and these details help to connect the audience to the presentation. Relevant examples or stories work to interest the listener and further develop main ideas.
2 The presenter provides basic information necessary for the audience to understand and enjoy the presentation. Stories and examples relate to the content of the speech.
1 The presenter does not support the ideas with additional information or explanation. Stories and examples are missing or unrelated.

R is for Responsive.

3 The presenter has matched the content of the presentation with the interests and/or needs of the audience.
2 The presenter has attempted to match the content of the presentation with the interests and needs of the audience.
1 Little thought has been given to the interests and needs of the audience.

How to Support Research

Our questions

Our thinking or hypotheses

How we are going to record what we find out

Ongoing questions as we work

How we want to tell others about our learning process

How we want to represent our learning findings

4

How to Make a Crowded Curriculum Work — Integration

Life Seen Whole

"Interdisciplinary teaching... is instruction that emphasizes the connections, the interrelations, among various areas of knowledge. In its broadest sense it is designed to help students 'to see life whole,' to integrate and make sense out of the myriad experiences they have, both in school and in the world at large."
— Gordon F. Vars and James A. Beane, *Interactive Curriculum in a Standards-Based World*, page 1

Olavi Mertanen, a researcher for the Helsinki-based Playful Learning Center project, describes Finland as "the leading country in terms of playful solutions to children's learning." You can read more about the revolution in education in Finland at http://www.zmescience.com/science/finland-education-system-25032015/#ixzz3dcGMejyv.

Many people who write about curriculum integration talk about the respect that needs to reside in the room as people work together to create innovative teaching. There is another kind of respect, as well: the respect for the knowledge and skills that the curriculum offers. Crucial to this work is finding the robustness of the tasks, the skillful scaffolding of one activity into another, and the refusal to water the curriculum down.

Curriculum integration allows teachers to find authentic, rather than forced ways of connecting various aspects of the curriculum. Content, knowledge, themes, relationships, and ways of knowing can be drawn from one discipline and used to enrich and apply to another. Various aspects of separate subject learning can be brought into meaningful associations through planned projects that carefully and skillfully integrate curriculum areas.

Integration allows us to teach in a way that makes sense to students, with inquiry as part of the process. Students are encouraged to ask questions, see different perspectives, connect facts and figures, think critically and imaginatively about ideas, work with materials in a variety of ways, and produce oral, written, mathematical, scientific, artistic, dramatic, and musical pieces in a way that has an authentic, real-world feel.

As I write this book, the education world is watching as the Finnish education authority takes a big leap. Finland is adopting what they are calling "phenomenon teaching." Finnish teachers are largely dispensing with the idea of teaching by classic school subjects in favor of teaching by broader topics across several subjects. I think the Finnish experiment takes education in a direction that encourages not only student engagement but also student autonomy. It is a brave step. It will be interesting to see how departments of education around the world respond to it.

To teach in the way being adopted by Finland, teachers often work collaboratively, mapping out their plans so that they can find connections among subjects. They begin by identifying themes, brainstorming relationships between ideas, and then drawing literal and figurative lines between different kinds of knowledge. Indeed, teaching in an integrated fashion requires not only various kinds of approaches but also different ways of thinking about the curriculum and its implementation. Teaching in this way has benefits for students. Integrated inquiry learning gives voice and choice to students. Students are given ownership of the assessment process and work towards representing what they are learning in a way that encourages creativity.

Teachers need multiple models of teaching in this way so that they can weave something new from many different threads. Through *Children's Minds, Talking Rabbits, and Clockwork Oranges: Essays on Education*, Kieran Egan (1999) has

The Examining of Relationships

"The focus of holistic education is on relationships — the relationship between linear thinking and intuition, the relationship between mind and body, the relationships between various domains of knowledge, the relationship between the individual and community.... In the holistic curriculum the student examines these relationships so that he/she gains both an awareness of them and the skills necessary to transform the relationships where it is appropriate."
— John P. Miller, *The Holistic Curriculum*, page 3

See "Planning an Integrated Unit: Questions to Guide You," a line master on pages 104 and 105.

helped me see that teachers need time to think about relationships that exist in the learning dynamic and plan ways to weave an integrated tapestry of teaching and learning together. For instance, Egan has helped me understand that to think musically is to think with and through patterned sound; to create music, students work with the expressive properties of sound. When students think mathematically, they imagine how quantitative relationships can be represented, explained, and displayed. Historical thinking allows students to create narratives composed of time, episodes, relationships, choices, consequences, and distance. To think dramatically is to consider other people's realities — to think and feel simultaneously about oneself in relation to other people and the stories they are living through in role.

Planning with Integration in Mind

In order for this kind of teaching to happen, teachers need to be given permission and support by the administrators in their schools to do the visioning, planning, scheduling, and implementing required. In the *All I's on Education* project, the research team and I spent two full-day planning meetings with the teachers, often including the principal, talking about the contexts of the learning environments, sharing their own identities and those of the students, understanding the culture of the school, and imagining how the curriculum could be developed in integrated ways. These potent discussions allowed all of us to share who we were, what we had experienced as educators, what our subject knowledge was, and the kinds of educational issues we cared about. We spent time brainstorming and dreaming, often starting at one point and ending at another. Each person in the planning group brought a different perspective, different experiences, different skill sets, and a different purpose, making the conversations rich, varied, challenging, and exciting. The compatibility of teachers to teachers, teachers to subjects, subjects to subjects, and teachers to students was a key component of these planning meetings.

As teachers begin to work together, they tell stories of what they know and then ask one another questions about how they can make the integrated unit work. In this way, they begin to see curriculum connections and convergences and can explore concepts and content that overlap and interconnect in interesting ways. They are intent on creating a rich tapestry of learning experiences that coincide. The colorful curriculum threads are designed in such a way that the learning experiences are unique and unpredictable. Some of the threads look random at certain points, but over time the purpose to the work emerges in the pattern of the evolving tapestry. There is an aesthetic to the plan, although sometimes the form is invisible. There is also an improvisational nature to the work, and teachers become very engaged because they want to see how the tapestry will develop.

Of course, this kind of work cannot happen unless the teachers are confident about their teaching and willing to risk failure to see different results. There also needs to be a fair degree of trust, collaboration, and respect among the teachers and their administrators. Collaboration requires a whole set of skills on the part of teachers and principals — a generosity of spirit that brings people together to create innovative curriculum that will make a difference in the learning lives of students and the teaching lives of teachers.

> "To create learning organizations, we must understand the underlying agreements we have made about how we will be together."
> — Margaret Wheatley

In my experience, collaboration is not always easy. The support that teachers receive from one another can be transformational on many levels, but sometimes co-teaching and co-planning seem like a burden. Time as well as timing can be an issue, and the brainstorming, sharing, and implementation of ideas can also be a challenge. Participants sometimes worry that they might dominate conversations, shut others down, or not tell their entire story. Others are less conscious than they might be of how they are presenting themselves in a group. They dominate, fail to listen, or refuse to give up what they view as ideas that have worked well in their classrooms. That is why establishing norms of engagement among working teams is important.

Norms of Engagement

Individual ownership and personal commitment are important aspects of group functioning. Although I never want to belabor the elements of group process, I find it is sometimes necessary to have people commit to certain agreements that might make the group function well. My colleague Ramon St. Vicente, at the Toronto District School Board, works with teachers in social justice education. Here are the four agreements he asks for when he and his colleagues embark upon discussions about equity education. I think that the same agreements can apply when we begin "courageous conversations" about collaborative teaching:

1. Stay engaged.
2. Speak your truth.
3. Experience discomfort.
4. Expect and accept non-closure.

Ways to approach integration

In my work, I have recognized four key aspects of how teachers might approach integration in their classrooms. They can adopt an integrating *theme*, for example, oppression or disappearance — the theme is likely what will drive the unit no matter its shape or scope. They can integrate *within* a subject, perhaps by having students read, write, speak, listen, and view in Language Arts, all to explore an overarching theme. Depending on their situation, teachers can plan to integrate *across* subjects, for example, creating a unit that combines work in Language Arts and Visual Arts or History and Drama. Finally, time and opportunity permitting, they can allow students to explore a theme both by integrating within a subject and by integrating across a number of subjects — improvising as they go along. Especially in this last case, integration becomes more like a tapestry than a quilt.

No matter how teachers decide to integrate, they will be
- opening up alternative approaches for learning, teaching, and communication for their students
- connecting course content, themes, concepts, and skills
- reducing the number of classroom transitions that happen in the school day
- addressing the multiple intelligences or learning styles of the students and allowing for more instruction time to explore various ideas
- developing avenues for expression not limited to words and numbers
- fostering relationships among teaching staff, students, and the community

How the planning stage develops is important. I once ran a workshop about curriculum integration called "No Forced Links, Just a Blend of Narratives." There I emphasized that teachers must be sure not to make superficial associations and to force curriculum connections when resistance emerges. If the integration seems too difficult, the connections may not make sense to the students. It takes a fair amount of effort and a lot of imagination and lengthy conversations to get really rich integrated units going.

Exploring the Potential of Themes

Finding a theme that links various disciplines allows learners to develop their thinking about important ideas. Some call these "big ideas." Themes can open us up to new ways of thinking about the world.

Here are some themes I have worked with in classrooms over the last several years:

journeys	dealing with family conflict
lost time	loss of identity
home	looking at the overlooked
perspective	not being able to go home
resistance	being banished
bridges	not being able to leave the house
abandonment	living on the margins
oppression	loss of innocence
disappearance	relationships worn thin
vulnerability	the constant feeling of irrelevance
imprisonment	turning away from someone
cyber-bullying	memorials
going green: environmental sustainability	the sense of not being able to stop things from happening
being stigmatized	

See the discussion on an integrated unit on the theme of lost time on pages 75 and 76.

From Color to Conservation
One primary classroom I worked in explored the theme of "going green." The class first spent time working with the color green and then moved into what *green* means in terms of sustainability.

Teachers choose a theme and then organize their teaching of various subjects around that theme. One way to work with themes is to transform them into big questions, such as these:
- What does *home* mean to different people?
- How can oppressed people ever forgive their oppressors?
- What would happen to the natural and human world if this forest ceased to exist?

Themes can also be connected to famous quotations. One could begin to think about the theme of isolation — or community — through John Donne's "No man is an island entire of itself." The theme of misunderstanding could be introduced by this Rudyard Kipling quotation, which comes from *The Light That Failed*: "We are all islands shouting lies to each other across seas of misunderstanding."

Themes can be broadened to encompass emotions associated with them, perhaps regret, surprise, pride, and feeling trapped. What's more, there are ways to group ideas and feelings together so that the learning can be multi-dimensional. Here are a few examples:

- home, journeys, risk, *fear*, and *hope*
- oppression, resistance, injustice, voice, *disappointment*, *anger*, and *intolerance*
- disappearance, appearance, loss, *surprise*, and *regret*

In this approach, it is easy to consider learning as a tapestry with layered threads.

Evolution of a theme-based unit: Lost time

In one school where I have worked, the teacher of a Grade 4 class wanted to do an integrated unit on the theme of time. The notes that she brought to the meeting included wonderful ideas that would allow her and her students to learn about math, science, history, and drama while pursuing the theme.

Museum as Frame: We needed to find a way to frame the unit so that it could work. After much discussion, we came up with the idea of a museum of lost time. Who and what would be represented in the museum? There could be stories of people who had lost track of time and stories of time travel. Students could be prompted to project many years forward and write a letter or piece of advice to their much older selves. They could investigate how time was read in the past. Their inquiry would focus on how sundials, shadow clocks, and stone circles helped ancient people read time and so on. Because these ancient technologies relied upon the sun and the moon literally "telling time," the connections to mathematics teaching of angles and intervals seemed natural. Although tempted to move into the realm of shadows — and take the unit into a different realm — in the end, we settled on lost time.

Tools of Time: How to expand the unit into the arts began to take shape, as well. We had thought of having the students design and create a number of time machines so that they could imagine going back in time to "capture" time. For the museum of lost time, the students could create and install three-dimensional timepieces, write about their importance and influence, and then demonstrate how the timepieces worked. They also crafted invitations for their parents and community members to see the museum.

Math and Science Infusion: The students were engaged in math and science work as they created their timepieces in small groups. The teacher was intent on integrating pulleys and gears, intervals, counting, and number sense into the project. She took time to help students gain hands-on experience.

Timepiece Display: The visual arts component was very rewarding as the students chose the medium that they would use to create their timepieces. They worked out the design on paper and then created their pieces using cardboard, Plasticine, newspaper, papier mâché, Lego, or found objects. Paint, glitter, buttons, feathers, pipe cleaners, hooks, and other small gadgets were all part of the design, and the students worked hard to make their pieces functional as well as beautiful.

The teacher challenged the students to find effective ways to place the timepieces in the museum. The students considered questions like these: Which pieces would look good together? How could the museum visitors really enjoy the space? How could the visit to the museum work in terms of flow? Through this experience, they learned how to create an art installation.

From History and Mystery to Drama: Then, as we did our research, we came across a mystery story related to time. The L. A. Mayer Museum for Islamic Art in Jerusalem had presented an exhibit called "The Mystery of Lost Time,"

Discovering rich potential is what is so lovely about working this way. You begin with one idea and then realize that there are many avenues to pursue.

A Way to Discover Uniqueness
"Art has the role in education of helping children become more themselves instead of more like everyone else."
— Sydney Gurewitz Clemens, *Art in the Classroom* (blog)

an exhibition of clocks and watches from the personal collection of Sir David Solomon. Many of the timepieces were the work of a brilliant Swiss horologist, Abraham-Louis Breguet, who revolutionized watchmaking. Breguet essentially invented the wristwatch centuries before it became fashionable and personally designed timepieces for Louis XVI and Marie Antoinette of France.

But it was the following story that enabled us to see how we could integrate some drama into the unit: in 1983, the entire collection of timepieces was stolen; later, on his deathbed, the thief confessed to his crime, and the collection was restored. We thought that the Grade 4 students would find the story compelling and want to do some imaginings to find out more.

When I worked with the students, I told them the story. We talked for a while about what it must have been like for the security guard to walk into the museum and find that everything had disappeared. We wondered why someone would steal a collection of timepieces. We brainstormed a list of people who might know the backstory, and the students suggested that the thief's wife might know a lot.

Backstory Imagining: I got the students into groups to develop questions that they might ask the wife in a hot-seating situation, in this case, with the teacher in role. The students used the same template that was introduced in Chapter 3 of this book. These are questions the students created:
- What was the name of your husband?
- How long were you married?
- Do you recall why he was so fascinated by these watches?
- Why do you think that your husband decided to steal the entire collection of watches?
- How did he do it?
- Where did he keep the stolen timepieces?
- How did he keep them hidden?
- Were you aware of their presence during the last number of years?
- Were you ever tempted to tell the police what he had done?
- Why did you protect him?
- Did you consider what he did was wrong?
- Why do you think that your husband finally confessed to the crime?
- What was his punishment?

Thus, what began as a unit based on the theme of time evolved into a unit encompassing math (angles and intervals), science (pulleys and gears, ancient technologies), story, letter, and invitation writing, art (time-travel machines and museum display), and drama (wondering about the mysterious theft). As often happens, the theme-based unit grew into a unit encompassing integration within and across subjects.

Images of Snow: Integrating by Theme within a Subject

The following closely related series of exercises allows teachers to integrate the Language Arts strands of reading, writing, listening, speaking, and viewing. I once facilitated this exercise with teachers of Intermediate/Senior students at a Reading for the Love of It workshop in Toronto. I did so in the middle of February during a snowstorm. The exercise seemed to fit with the theme of the conference because the words in all of the excerpts used paint a picture of snow that is unique, beautiful, and compelling and allow students to fall in love with language. The exercise or one based on the same principle can be implemented in similar ways at any time.

1. *I See, I Remember, I Imagine:* I projected a painting of a snowy Montréal street by John Little and asked participants to record everything they saw in the painting, everything that the painting reminded them of, and how the painting helped them imagine other snow scenes. As a sample, here is what one participant wrote:

    > *I see . . .*
    > Snow draping the trees
    > Different colours of snow
    > Skies of pink and grey
    > A feeling that more snow is coming soon
    > *I remember . . .*
    > Snowstorms when I was younger
    > The feeling of being glad to be home
    > One of my student's first snowfall and how all the children and I ran to the window to help him see
    > *I imagine . . .*
    > Snow falling in a dark wood at night
    > Snow piling up in my driveway at home
    > Footprints in the snow

2. *Modelled Reading and Active Listening:* I then handed out a copy of an excerpt from a scene in literature (see pages 78 and 79) and read it aloud. I read it again and then let the sounds of the words sit in the room. I then asked the teachers present to respond — I made sure to tell them that their response could simply be about the sound of the words, the feelings and memories evoked, or the way the image was created by the author.

    I read aloud a second carefully chosen excerpt just so the participants could hear another descriptive paragraph. I also elicited their response.

What Reading Aloud to Students Enables Them to Do

One way to engage your students in learning is to read aloud in the classroom. The time is well spent and renders positive results. Reading aloud creates a bond among the student listeners because they experience something together. It often causes significant changes in students' attitudes towards reading because it allows students to

- create images in their minds
- hear and see models of proficient reading
- listen to "good" writing
- build content-area background knowledge
- find pleasure in the experience
- hear language that they would not be aware of without this experience
- anticipate what will happen next and hone their skills of prediction
- fall in love with language

I chose my readings from the following, using the scene from Annie Dillard's *An American Childhood* first.

SCENE ONE: From *An American Childhood*, Annie Dillard
Now we sat in the dark dining room, hushed. The big snow outside, the big snow on the roof, silenced our words and the scrape of our forks and our chairs. The dog was gone, the world outside was dangerously cold, and the big snow held the houses down and the people in.

Behind me, tall chilled windows gave out onto the narrow front yard and the street. A motion must have caught my mother's eye; she rose and moved to the windows, and Father and I followed. There we saw the young girl, the transfigured Jo Ann Sheehy, skating alone under the streetlight.

She was turning on ice skates inside the streetlight's yellow cone of light — illumined and silent. She tilted and spun. She wore a short skirt, as if Edgerton Avenue's asphalt had been the ice of an Olympic arena. She wore mittens and a red knitted cap below which her black hair lifted when she turned. Under her skates the street's packed snow shone; it illumined her from below, the cold light striking her under her chin.

I stood at the tall window, barely reaching the sill; the glass fogged before my face, so I had to keep moving or hold my breath. What was she doing out there? Was everything beautiful so bold?

SCENE TWO: From *Ethan Frome*, Edith Wharton
But at sunset the clouds gathered again, bringing an earlier night, and the snow began to fall straight and steadily from a sky without wind, in a soft universal diffusion more confusing than the gusts and eddies of the morning. It seemed to be a part of the thickening darkness, to be the winter night itself descending on us layer by layer.

SCENE 3: From *The Dead*, James Joyce
A few light taps upon the pane made him turn to the window. It had begun to snow again. He watched sleepily the flakes, silver and dark, falling obliquely against the lamplight. The time had come for him to set out on his journey westward. Yes, the newspapers were right: snow was general all over Ireland. It was falling on every part of the dark central plain, on the treeless hills, falling softly upon the Bog of Allen and, farther westward, softly falling into the dark mutinous Shannon waves. It was falling, too, upon every part of the lonely churchyard on the hill where Michael Furey lay buried. It lay thickly drifted on the crooked crosses and headstones, on the spears of the little gate, on the barren thorns. His soul swooned slowly as he heard the snow falling faintly through the universe and faintly falling, like the descent of their last end, upon all the living and the dead.

SCENE 4: From *The Magic Mountain*, Thomas Mann (Trans. John E. Woods)

Usually the snow stopped at that hour of the day, as if for a quick survey of what had been achieved thus far; the rare days of sunshine seemed to serve much the same purpose — the flurries died down and the sun's direct glare attempted to melt the luscious, pure surface of drifted new snow. It was a fairy-tale world, child-like and funny. Boughs of trees adorned with thick pillows, so fluffy someone must have plumped them up; the ground a series of humps and mounds, beneath which slinking underbrush or outcrops of rock lay hidden; a landscape of crouching, cowering gnomes in droll disguises — it was comic to behold, straight out of a book of fairy tales.

> When I work with students, reading along with them, I can listen in informally to their oral reading without putting them on the spot.

3. *Walk-Around Reading:* I handed out one of the four texts I was featuring to each of the participants and asked them to stand up. I told them that when touched on the shoulder, they were to walk around the classroom reading the text out loud. They were to concentrate on reading the text and not make eye contact with anyone. They had to be careful not to bump into anyone or into the chairs as they walked and read (if the group is large, it can be split into two). I also told them that when they got to the end of the story, they were to return to the beginning and read again. The participants walked and read for a few minutes. I read along with them.

   Then, as if they were students in the classroom, I asked the participants to "freeze" and prompted them to spend a moment finding the line, word, or phrase that most captured their imagination or affected them in some way. Perhaps they liked the way that the words "spring off the page," found the image a line evoked for them dramatic, considered a line personally important, or liked the way a phrase sounded as they read it out loud.

   I gave the workshop participants a few minutes and then asked them to continue walking, saying that line out loud over and over. They had a chance to practice using their projected voices before the next part of the activity. I asked everyone to freeze again. I told them that when I touched them on the shoulder, they were to say the word, line, or phrase out loud. They were to say it again if I indicated for them to do so. I played soft music, and then we began to create our own out-loud reading of the text.

   Here is what it sounded like:

   > The big snow.
   > The big snow
   > Held the houses down and the people in.
   > The world outside was dangerously cold.
   > Hushed,
   > Illumined and silent.
   > The street's packed snow shone.
   > Was everything beautiful so bold?
   > So bold?

4. *Paint Me a Paragraph:* I followed Walk-Around Reading with this exercise, which works very well with students in the classroom too. The exercise

requires critical literacy and group co-operation and decision making. It is also wonderful for vocabulary building.

To do it, have students work with a partner or in groups of three. Hand out five or six paint chips per group. If students do not know the meaning of the word on the paint chip (e.g., *roadster*), have them look it up.

Put the following paragraph on an overhead screen or Smart Board:

> The _____ snow was getting heavier now, swirling down in great flurries over the silent _____ city, purposefully filling everyone's boot-shaped imprints, making them _____. The _____ streets were empty, still immersed in late December twilight. The trees were dressed in _____ snow that lay innocently on their branches. The wind whistled in a strange way, making Ivor shiver but he did not know why.

Exploring Words in a Range of Ways

"Taking the words and exploring them verbally, visually and kinesthetically enables children to access the written text using a wider range of intelligences and learning styles."
— Patrice Baldwin and Kate Fleming, *Teaching Literacy through Drama: Creative Approaches*, page 20

Have the students see if they can find a way to add most of the paint chip language into the paragraph (typically they are given six chips to consider for five blanks). For instance, one group worked with the following paint chips: silhouette white; paper white; satchel brown; palest pistachio; gray lake; foggy. This is what the group came up with:

> The **paper white** snow was getting heavier now, swirling down in great flurries over the silent **satchel brown** city, purposefully filling everyone's boot-shaped imprints, making them **silhouette white**. The **foggy** streets were empty, still immersed in late December twilight. The trees were dressed in (the) **palest pistachio** snow that lay innocently on their branches. The wind whistled in a strange way, making Ivor shiver but he did not know why.

Another group worked with paint chips featuring these words: simply white; lemon sorbet; tranquility; Chantilly lace; ancient ivory; chestnut brown. This is what that group came up with:

> The **lemon sorbet** snow was getting heavier now, swirling down in great flurries over the silent **chestnut brown** city, purposefully filling everyone's boot-shaped imprints, making them **simply white**. The **ancient ivory** streets were empty, still immersed in late December twilight. The trees were dressed in **Chantilly lace** ~~snow~~ that lay innocently on their branches. The wind whistled in a strange way, making Ivor shiver but he did not know why.

Students are allowed to make only one independent change in the paragraph — that is, they could cut or add one word.

A graphic novel by Hervé Bouchard and Janice Nadeau, Harvey, offers a delightful description of a muddy spring. I have used this excerpt and paint chips to have students write about Spring.

When doing this exercise with students, ask two groups to compare their paragraphs and consider these questions: "What new words did you learn? What were the best images? What seemed forced?"

Paint Chip Potential: There are many ways to extend this exercise into responses and representations through dance, visual arts, reading, and writing. Students could find ways of interpreting their snow paragraphs through improvised movement to music; sketch responses to the paragraphs that have been created by the class and create a class mural; or respond to other texts about seasons and weather.

Leaving Home: Integrating by Theme and across Subjects

In this section two quite different approaches to exploring the theme of leaving home are taken. The first uses visual art as the initial stimulus to consider the experiences of Indigenous children, forced to attend residential schools where they largely lost their language and culture. The second helps students understand how the French-speaking Acadians must have felt when forced by their British conquerors to leave their homes at short notice. Various drama techniques were employed to help achieve this.

The Story Must Now Be Told — Residential schools

Studying Artistic Images: Show students a series of slides of photographs, paintings, and sculptures. Ten to 12 pieces should be enough. You will want to have a wide variety of images, including historical photographs and contemporary art, in this case, related to the students' growing understanding of the impact of residential schools on First Nations, Inuit, and Métis students and their families. Some students might respond to the artistic images with a fair bit of knowledge. Others might not. This activity is a way for you to gauge what your students know about this topic.

Show the slide show again — this time very slowly.

Show the slide show a third time, asking students to discover the slide that affects them the most.

Critiquing Art: Once they identify the slide that has the most impact on them, students are to stop you at that moment so they can explain why the slide has this effect on them. Help the students to use artistic language as they talk. You may want to introduce them to words and concepts such as *design, focus, color, pattern, foreground, background, intensity, movement, light, balance, form, feeling, juxtaposition, surprise*, and *contrast*.

Capturing Elements: Ask students to form groups of four. Hand each group a large sheet of paper and tell them to fold it into a four-square grid. Have students sit in front of their part of the paper and close their eyes. Invite them to think about the piece of art that they chose and focus on the element that caught their attention the most. Tell them that when they open their eyes, they can use the materials (e.g., colored markers, crayons, bits of fabric, feathers, and buttons) at the front of the classroom to capture that element in some distinct way. They are not going to reproduce the painting, photograph, or sculpture; instead, they will create something new from what they saw. So, they might, for example, decide to draw a face or a pattern or create a series of squiggles or lines.

Making a Collaborative Creation: Once they have created individual pieces, have all four students in each group stand back and look at what they have created. Ask them:
- What visual arts elements are present?
- What is the overall effect of the piece?
- Is there anything that could be done to the creation to give it more of a form, or is it better left the way it is?
- Does the piece that combines four different artistic interpretations have a sense of unity? What could be altered so that it has that kind of effect?
- Is there a message in the piece that is discoverable only now? What kind of message is it?
- How does talking about the artistic piece and the artistic choices you made help you understand the effect of residential schools on children and their families?

Refining Interpretations: Prompt the students to discuss their ideas and come to an agreement of what to do. Once they have done so, they can go back and make adjustments, as necessary. For example, they might decide to cut up their piece and place the four interpretations in a linear manner or focus on certain parts of the various interpretations and combine them to create a kind of flow or interesting juxtapositions of colors and shapes. They might also write poetry based on what they have created, give their collaboration a title, and display it in the classroom or somewhere else in the school.

Exploring the Statement of Reconciliation: The collaborative artwork activity just outlined can be used in a variety of contexts, one of which is as part of a theme-based integrated unit on being forced to leave home. In one instance, I was working with Grade 8 students learning about the impact of residential schools on members of Canada's Indigenous peoples. After the students had produced collaborative art, I began to expose them to text sources.

I read aloud an excerpt from the Canadian government's 1998 "Statement of Reconciliation," which appears in *Gathering Strength — Canada's Aboriginal Action Plan*, and then projected the statement on the Smart Board. The students worked in groups of five to respond to what they had heard and read, coming up with notes and questions.

> **Excerpt from the Statement of Reconciliation**
> Sadly, our history with respect to the treatment of Aboriginal people is not something in which we can take pride. Attitudes of racial and cultural superiority led to a suppression of Aboriginal culture and values. As a country, we are burdened by past actions that resulted in weakening the identity of Aboriginal peoples, suppressing their languages and cultures, and outlawing spiritual practices. We must recognize the impact of these actions on the once self-sustaining nations that were disaggregated, disrupted, limited or even destroyed by the dispossession of traditional territory, by the relocation of Aboriginal people, and by some provisions of the Indian Act. We must acknowledge that the result of these actions was the erosion of the political, economic and social systems of Aboriginal people and nations.

Learning from Personal Primary Sources: I then invited the students to imagine what it must have been like for very young children to leave their homes and communities to attend residential schools. I handed out excerpts from Shirley Sterling's *My Name Is Seepeetza*, an autobiographical novel in diary form about the author's experiences at Kalamak Indian Residential School in the 1950s. Earlier, the classroom teacher had read the book's beginning. I directed the students as follows: "Let's try to imagine how Seepeetza and her family felt about her having to leave home to go so far away to school. Using your excerpt and the art materials you have been given, see if you can capture that experience through art making."

Making Artistic Representations: Using the same collaborative art-making format as described above, the groups each created a panel of artistic response to Seepeetza's story. When they shared their panels with the rest of the class, the teacher and I asked the class to see if they could put the artwork into some kind of chronology based on the feelings, images, colors, and so on. The students found this to be a challenge.

Imagining a Gallery Exhibit: Once we had some sort of chronology, we stepped back from the artwork. I asked, "If we were going to install these pieces in an art gallery and advertise it to the public, what kinds of words would we use on the front of the brochure to inform people of the kind of work that they would see?"

The students came up with various titles for the exhibition, for example, Hallways of Shame, The Sadness of Leaving, and The Story Must Now Be Told.

Potential for Art and Voices Combined: Although there was no time to create the brochure, I felt that this would have been a powerful culminating activity — integrating visual arts, history, technology, current affairs, and language arts. Students could create the front cover of the brochure and then add historical information juxtaposed to the artwork that they had created. They could research the stories from the Truth and Reconciliation Commission of Canada and excerpt quotations from people whose voices were just now being heard.

I always feel that time is one of a teacher's biggest enemies. We all have ideas of how a unit could be expanded, but often we have to abandon the work because of time constraints. My suggestion for teachers is to keep a journal of the ideas that are left behind. There might be another time and place when these tantalizing ideas could be implemented.

The Acadian Expulsion — Bringing history home through drama

At York University, one major assignment I give to my pre-service teacher candidates is to create a history and drama unit titled "What It Must Have Been Like." Students work in small groups researching historical material based on a specific theme connected to the Ontario History curriculum at the Grade 7 or 8 level. Among the topics are the building of the Canadian Pacific Railway, the Acadian Expulsion, the Underground Railroad, and the settlement of the West.

As the students research material that has potential for dramatic exploration, they participate in inquiry-based learning by addressing this question:

> What must it have been like for a person or group of persons who
> lived during that time, in that place, in those conditions, under those
> circumstances?

They then prepare and present part of a drama unit to the class, allowing them to experience learning about history through drama. Participants understand "what it must have been like" by "living through" the imagined historical context of fictional characters based on historical research.

Depending on choice of strategies, a dramatic exploration of the Acadian Expulsion (1755–62) could allow students to gain a sense of what the Expulsion meant to Acadian families. During the Seven Years' War, otherwise known as the French and Indian War, the French-speaking families living in what is now Nova Scotia were expelled from their homes and shipped to what is now the eastern seaboard of the United States or to France or England.

Into Role as Family Members: Students were asked to work in groups and become members of Acadian families. Each group was given a family name and asked to determine who they were within the family. Since each family member had to be old enough to talk about the issues, everyone had to represent someone more than five years old. The family names were Le Breton, Champagne, Langevin, Tranchemontagne, and Beaumont.

Students set about researching how the Acadians might have lived under British rule (e.g., planting and harvesting crops, repairing dykes, shearing sheep, salting meat, cutting firewood, building furniture, preserving food, making clothes, milking cows, weaving).

Speaking in Role: Later, in order to portray a typical day in the life of the Acadians, the students in small groups created a tableau and a short monologue that would give others a sense of the strong connection they had to their home and the land. For each group's tableau, I touched students on the shoulder, and one by one, they spoke in role about the work they were doing. For example, a student said: "My name is Francine Tranchemontagne. I am weaving a blanket from the wool that we have from our sheep. Everything I do is connected to the land. My husband, my parents, and my children all work together to survive the harsh realities of living on the land."

Assembling the Acadians: I told the students in their family groups that they had been summoned to attend an important meeting in the local church at 4 o'clock. They were to bring all their family members.

Before we negotiated the way the families would enter the space, we talked about the reaction that the Acadians would have to this summons. Would they have had a premonition of what was going to happen? How would they be feeling? What could they do or say that would change what would happen next? We then talked about how they would enter the church. Would they sit as families? Would each family enter at a different time? Would they greet one another? Would they enter in silence? We discussed what they thought might happen.

We set up the classroom the way that a church might look with an aisle down the center. On a signal from me and with a request that everyone remain silent, the families entered the space and sat, and I handed out to each family a copy of an Expulsion Notice (an abridgment of a historical document). They read it silently. I decided to play the role of a British soldier (although a priest serving as intermediary also works well). I read the notice out loud and said:

> You have been read the notice. There is a limited time for questions. You will be required to return to your homes and retrieve only those possessions that you can carry with you on the ship. Please do not bring any furniture or pets. There will be limited room.

A Day in the Life
As part of establishing a day in the life of an Acadian family, the class could create a series of tableaux. Prompt the students to imagine what happens at first light, morning, noon, afternoon, and evening. Invite them to consider how a day in family life would be different during each of the four seasons.

A translation of the original document by Brigadier-General Charles Lawrence can be found at www.danielnpaul.com/AcadienExpulsion-1755.html.

The students were allowed to ask a few questions, and then the role playing stopped. We discussed the kinds of possessions that the Acadians would want to take with them.

Writing in Role as Family Artifacts: I laid out objects such as those listed below in the middle of the classroom and told the students that they represented cherished possessions left behind when the Acadians were expelled. Many of them were found on the beach years later. The students gathered around, and each group chose an object. They could talk among themselves to decide which one to take, determining what the artifact signified.

a silver candlestick	a piece of pottery
a lace wedding veil	a shoe buckle
a tea cup	a pocket knife
a silver spoon	a map
a leather-bound notebook	a tin cup
a quill pen	a small brooch
an apron	a handkerchief
a small painting	

Groups could decide whether to accompany their presentation with music. "Nimrod" by Edward Elgar, for example, would be an appropriate choice.

The students worked together in their groups, creating the story behind the artifact that they had chosen. Each group wrote the story on an index card, and one member volunteered to speak as that object. Other group members coached the volunteer.

This sample piece of writing was composed by a group of teacher candidates.

A SMALL BROOCH

At one time I was polished weekly and worn on a meticulously pressed lace collar proudly displayed for all to see. Now I lay hidden, tarnished and abandoned in a jewellery box that was tossed aside because the looters could not break the lock. I am a witness to the devastation caused by the British. I remember the day they took them all away . . .

Caught in a Rumor Mill: After showing students a short YouTube film on the Acadian Expulsion (https://www.youtube.com/watch?v=RnpW5IVyWtU), I said: "Imagine what must be going on in the minds of the families that are being forced from their homes. They are in a crisis, and often when this happens, a community becomes rife with worry and gossip. What must it have been like on the days leading up to the Expulsion? What would the Acadians have been whispering to one another about?"

I prompted the students to create a rumor mill, where, as Acadians, they walked around the space but froze whenever directed to. When touched on the shoulder, a student would say in a stage whisper what he or she had overheard, always starting with "I heard that . . ."

> I heard that they are going to separate the men from the women.
> I heard that they will kill us if we do not do what they say.
> I heard that all of us have to meet Governor Lawrence in the church at 3 o'clock.

I created an orchestration of whispered voices, sometimes repeated. I was trying to tap into the emotion of the moment of these families leaving their cherished homes. Using whispers heightened the experience because students were required to really listen to the evolving symphony of sadness and worry. This kind of work obliges the teacher to remember who said what and to scaffold the voices in such a way that a powerful experience — a kind of vocal tapestry — can be created in the classroom.

Reflection: After the exercise was over, the students and I discussed these questions:

- What did it feel like to hear the whispered worries of a people who were being expelled from the land that had been part of their ancestry?
- Can you describe a particular moment that resonated with you?
- What feelings are associated with this kind of oppression?
- Whose voices did we not hear? Why were they silenced?
- If we had heard the voices of the British soldiers, how would that have changed the experience?

Bodystorming: To each "family group" I handed out a copy of a notice (found at http://www.acadian.org/st-j-val.html):

> On a fateful day in 1755, the people were summoned to the church, by order of Governor Lawrence. Not suspecting any treachery, they went in, and the doors were locked at once. A proclamation was read to the effect that they were prisoners of the King and that they would be deported. All their lands were confiscated, and some of the houses and barns were set on fire. At the point of the bayonet, they were ushered to the boats that were waiting for them, to take them away and scatter them along the Atlantic Coast. Directions were given on the manner they should behave in the new country to which they were being taken. Husbands, wives and children were separated for fear some might venture to come back and settle nearby. They were put on different boats, some being taken to Boston, others to Louisiana, and still others to Bermuda.

Bodystorming Tips

- As in brainstorming, there is no editing of ideas in the bodystorming process. All movement ideas are encouraged and welcomed. If the students are to create a movement piece, they will then begin to negotiate what to use and how to string their movement ideas together.
- Remind the students that they are not to use words to describe their idea, but to show their classmates in movement.

The struggle depicted in the YouTube video, noted earlier, is understated in many ways, and there is little dialogue; however, students could see the way in which the Acadians were put onto separate boats and sent on their way. They could begin to imagine what the Acadians were feeling, thinking, and experiencing as they were deported. One way to explore these feelings and thoughts is to have students "bodystorm."

Bodystorming, in essence, is much like brainstorming but uses the body as a means of exploring and communicating the movement possibilities linked to the themes, issues, and ideas that students may be exploring. It is a way for students to engage the elements of movement — body, space, relationship, and quality — as they work. The strategy encourages students to explore their movement ideas, and the ideas of others, with depth and authenticity.

The whole class explored a range of movements based on the concept of Acadian resistance to their expulsion. The students stood in a circle and, one at a time, shared their movement interpretation of the concept of "resistance." Everyone as a group then repeated each student's work. I encouraged the students to build on this movement, taking it into a new direction by changing, for example, the level or the tempo or moving a different body part.

Students then worked in small groups or partners to generate a pool of movement ideas. In this context, they negotiated movement ideas attached to such words as *anger, sadness, dismay, resistance,* and *betrayal.* They chose the words and movements most meaningful to them and tried to express clearly the essence of their ideas through their bodies.

If time permits...

There are many ways in which a unit like the Acadian unit could be developed further. All depend on time. Here are some suggestions:

If the Walls Could Speak: Have students imagine what the walls of the abandoned houses would say after the expulsion of the Acadians. What were the last moments like? Was anyone left behind? Did anyone hide in the forest? Let the walls remember what happened by speaking a few lines.

Back and Forth Letters: Have students write letters in role as the women or men on the separate ships. After the students have completed their writing, prompt them to underline the most powerful line. You could orchestrate a reading of these lines back and forth across the classroom.

What Was the Result? Have students research what happened to the Acadians. Where did they go? Did any of them ever return? What effect did the Expulsion have on a place like New Orleans?

Why teach history through drama

One of my students, Rachel Downansky, offered this thoughtful evaluation of teaching the Acadian Expulsion in the integrated way outlined above:

> Some of the challenges of teaching history through drama is also the most strengthening factor; more specifically, the human element. Because we cannot predict what our students will say while doing role work, the experience may take an unexpected turn which we, as teacher, cannot prepare for. Being caught off guard is only one challenge that arises from the human element. Another is the idea that teaching history does require some element of actual facts; otherwise, it turns into teaching English using a fictionalized piece of non-fiction... A pleasant surprise that occurred (this time and others) while teaching History through Drama is the thoughtfulness invoked by even the shyest and most withdrawn student; the moment when it becomes clear they are not disengaged, but deep in complex thought.

Below are three more responses from teacher-candidate students who experienced being taught history through drama, by their peers. The reflections point to the considerable value of integrating across subjects:

> Living through these stories — and having them be so "particular" — made me see my country in a different light. I now see that Canada is a country made up of the descendants of thousands of people who suffered at the hands of the more powerful. I now understand colo-

nialism. Never did before. So . . . this big concept is suddenly accessible through drama. Who would have thought? Now I get why drama can be a way into understanding not only human stories but systems of oppression. Exciting to think about doing this work in schools.
— Saeed

Preparing and teaching our history/drama lesson to our peers was intense but once I began to see the students engaged in "living through" a moment in the Expulsion of the Acadians as members of particular families, I was both moved and shaken. Watching each family pack their precious possessions and speak about each item was very powerful drama. It struck me afterwards how sad it is that most kids who study history in school never hear the voices of these people. They do not see the struggle of the people who fought against oppression. I am now more determined than ever to use drama in a cross-curricular way. This is powerful learning and complicated teaching.
— Don

Kathy always talks about hearing the "silent voices." When I first heard her say that, I did not know what she meant. Well, now I do because I heard them at last . . . It was so important to understand this by doing the work and pushing ourselves to take risks in our teaching.
— Bethany

Disappearance: Integrating by Theme, within Subjects, and across Subjects

"History is a symphony of echoes heard and unheard. It is a poem with events as verses."
— Charles Angoff

Over the years, as I have taught pre-service teachers and other teachers about inquiry, I developed the following model unit based on the theme of disappearance. This unit allows teachers to help students imagine what it must have been like to live in New France at the time *les filles du roi* arrived. It also allows teachers to integrate history, language arts, drama, visual arts, and music in seamless ways that are enlightening and intriguing.

Here is the inquiry question:

> How can invented, imaginary characters created in drama based on historical facts help students empathize with their predicament, comprehend their lives, and understand how their legacies shaped the future?

So much of history is about human emotions, the choices people make, and the relationships they enter into. Beyond curriculum, such as the Ontario Curriculum in Grade 7, asking that students "use a variety of resources and tools to gather, process, and communicate information about how settlers in New France met the physical, social, and economic challenges of the new land," I like to engage students in the emotional aspects of history. When they meet fictional characters who might have lived during the historical time, it allows them to understand more of history, culture, and society because they make personal connections.

The focus of the unit is on the historical phenomenon of *les filles du roi*, or the King's Daughters. These women arrived in the colony of New France, now the province of Quebec, between 1663 and 1673, under the financial sponsorship of King Louis XIV of France. There were 770 of them. They were single French women from various backgrounds, and many were orphans. Their purpose was to marry the unmarried male colonists in New France, have many children, and thus secure the settlement of the colony by populating it. In fact, 737 of these women did marry, and the ensuing population explosion was considered a success by the king of France and his ministers. (Most of the millions of people of French Canadian descent today — in Quebec, the rest of Canada, the United States, and even beyond! — are descendants of these courageous women.*)

The women captured my imagination: they disappeared from France only to show up again across an ocean on a different continent, in an unfamiliar environment, with little power and influence. As I work with students, we develop specific inquiry questions such as these:

> Why and how did these women leave France?
> What tricks of their personal fates allowed them to board a ship bound for New France alone and in the company of other women?
> What stories did these women bring with them?
> What kinds of lives did these women live in France?
> What kinds of oppression did they experience?
> What did they leave behind?
> What was the departure from their homeland like?
> What articles would they have been allowed to bring with them?
> How did they feel about their situation?
> What would the experience have been like on the ship?
> What did they do to survive the indignities of travel?
> How many died? How many survived?
> What was it like when they disembarked in New France?
> What happened to them on the first day?
> How do you think they would have felt about their circumstances?

We do not have answers to these questions and others like them except in our imaginations. The women's voices seem to have evaporated. There are church records of their marriages, but essentially — as is the case for so many women in all sorts of countries — the stories of their lives remain untold.

Beginning with an exploration of artifacts and ending with imaginings based on diary text, here is how I recommend structuring the unit:

How to Use Artifacts in Teaching

I use artifacts a lot in my teaching. I look for artifacts in antique stores, galleries, and other places, and I keep them in an old suitcase that also comes in handy in various teaching situations. I have a bunch of old keys, a number of colorful scarves, an assortment of old photographs, maps, the collar of a dress, a crumpled and disheveled antique puppet, stones with symbols on them, a clown's make-up kit, a hat pin, an old perfume bottle, a collection of very old letters, and a diary written by my great uncle during the First World War.

---

* http://www.fillesduroi.org/src/kings_daughters.htm (2010-0912).

> I carefully design my lessons so that artifacts are introduced at specific points to "hook" students into thinking about people, their stories, their relationships, and the choices they made.
>
> I use the artifacts in all sorts of different ways. I use them to introduce historical events, picture books, and new concepts; help students make their way through difficult texts; and trigger students' memories because they allow students to make connections with their personal experiences — to remember things about their lives that can inform their understanding of the lives of others who might be very different from them. The artifacts inspire discussion and debate.
>
> Students respond well to artifacts. They love the fact that they are allowed to touch the materials, pass them around the circle in small groups, wonder about their use or origin, link them to the characters and incidents in the books they are reading, and use them in their oral presentations to the rest of the class.

Engaging the Students — Working with Artifacts: I ask the class to get into groups of five and give one of the following artifacts to each group:

a locket (Anne)	a sketch of an old family home (Marguerite)
a needle and thread (Marie)	a Bible (Elize)
a torn quilt (Catherine)	a pouch of coins (Jeanne)

I then prompt the students to examine the artifact by passing it around the circle. I ask them: "What sorts of personal connections can you make with the object?" And then I tell them: "Each of these objects is very significant to the woman whose name is indicated on the card. It was the only thing that the woman was allowed to take with her on her voyage across the Atlantic. The object tells a little part of the story of the woman's past. The story may or may not be told ever again because the woman keeps the story locked in her heart."

Let the Artifact Speak — Writing in Role: Each group invents the backstory of the woman using the artifact. If the artifact could speak, what story would it tell us?

Here is what a few students have written:

ANNE'S LOCKET

> I am a locket that hangs around the neck of Anne, one of the King's daughters. In it is a picture of her only child — a child who was taken from her. Anne had been a servant in a large household in Paris and the child was illegitimate. Her employers fired her after they found out she was pregnant and Anne had to give her child up for adoption. For the past three months, Anne has lived on the streets. Because she is very beautiful, she was offered this opportunity to board the ship for New France. As her locket, I will try to protect her from the journey that lies ahead.

MARIE'S NEEDLE AND THREAD

I am the needle and thread that Marie keeps in her coat pocket. I remind her of happier times when she was employed as a seamstress in a shop that created beautiful dresses for aristocratic women. Marie fell on the ice last winter and broke both wrists. As a result she could not work and found herself in a poor house. The administrator of the poor house asked if she would be interested in going to New France once her wrists had healed. Marie felt that she had no other choice. Perhaps I can be useful on board ship as people tear their clothes on the journey. Perhaps the sails will need mending.

Once students in small groups have collaboratively written a piece, they hand it in for teacher feedback and assessment.

Setting the Space — Farewell to France: Each group uses their text and the artifact to imagine and then create the moment that the women boarded the ship that would carry them to New France. They decide where their particular woman would stand, how she would hold the artifact, and when the artifact would speak. The group could decide that all of them will speak as the artifact or coach one in the group to perform. All of the students then work with the other groups to create an improvised farewell scene in which the artifacts speak.

Tableaux Based on Messages in Bottles: Now I ask the students to get into groups of three and hand each group one of the messages shown below. I explain that each message has been found in a bottle washed up on a shore and tell them that the lines somehow relate to *les filles du roi*.

The students are to create a tableau of the context in which the woman found herself. So, participants use their bodies to create a "freeze frame" which captures a key moment, idea, reaction, statement, or theme. Once they have done so, they share their idea or moment with their classmates in complete stillness and silence.

Movement transitions may be used to connect a series of tableaux, and the images can be given titles or captions, or be brought to life for a few moments to allow the actors to say lines or speak in role. In this case, on a signal, the woman or sailor is to step out of the tableau and give a short monologue. The prompt line needs to be said somewhere within the monologue, and the rest of the group can earlier work with the speaker to help her or him express ideas authentically.

This strategy is extremely effective in helping students embody their understanding of texts.

Messages as Tableau Prompts

I did not want to leave you behind. I will never forget you.
Anne
Somewhere in the mid-Atlantic, July 18, 1663

As soon as we set sail, I realized what a horrible mistake I had made.
Bernadette
Somewhere in the mid-Atlantic, July 18, 1663

> *No money. No dowry. No hope.*
> *Jeanne*
> Somewhere in the mid-Atlantic, July 18, 1663
>
> *I think I am pregnant. Now what will happen to me? To us?*
> *Catherine*
> Somewhere in the mid-Atlantic, July 18, 1663
>
> *My hope lies across the sea. I will make a life — a life worth living.*
> *Marguerite*
> Somewhere in the mid-Atlantic, July 18, 1663
>
> *Some make it; some don't. They are all here for their own reasons.*
> *Sailor Jean*
> Somewhere in the mid-Atlantic, July 18, 1663
>
> *We try to make them as comfortable as possible, but it is not always easy.*
> *Sailor Michel*
> Somewhere in the mid-Atlantic, July 18, 1663
>
> *These women are cargo, just like everything else. And they bring a fair price with them.*
> *Captain*
> Somewhere in the mid-Atlantic, July 18, 1663

The Imagination as Gateway

"Dewey wrote that imagination was the gateway through which meanings derived from earlier experiences could find their way into present-day enactments. He said that present-day enactments become human and conscious to the degree that they are extended by meanings and values drawn from what is absent and present only imaginatively. When that happens, the past itself can be remade, even as the present becomes more luminous."
— Maxine Greene, *Variations on a Blue Guitar*, page 89

Relationships on Ship Visibly Conveyed: I now want the experience to become visible, visceral, and potent. I ask the students to think about the meaning concentrated in the figures of these women and men on board this ship sailing from France to New France in 1663. In small groups, they create a group of statues in which these characters freeze their bodies in ways that tell the story of their lives. I want them to enlarge and deepen the lives of these people by imagining what their bodies could tell us. The relationship of the women to each other, to the men on board the ship, to the atmosphere in the hold, or the weather on the deck needs to be created somehow — through costume, prop, light, color, or in some other way, including music or sound.

We then spend time looking at the constellations of relationships that are represented by each group and consider these questions:

- Why are the women huddled together so far away from the men?
- Why are the women looking inward and the men looking out to sea?
- What is the significance of the gestures, body language, and facial expressions of the statues?
- How can we feel, perceive, think, and imagine differently because of what we have just witnessed?
- How can this way of working in the body provide us with a way of knowing that is as powerful as the facts in a textbook?

The World through Lists: Sometimes, it is difficult for students to understand how different the world was hundreds of years ago. One way to have them imagine a past world is to have them list all the items that they take on a long journey. First, they can work in small groups, brainstorming all the things that they would want to bring if they were going on a journey today: loaded cell phone, toothbrush and toothpaste, return ticket, bottled water, passport, money, and so on.

I then have the students imagine that it is 1663 and that they are with *les filles du roi* on their journey. They work with a partner or in small groups, and cross off all the items that these women would not have. We then discuss what the women might have with them.

Consideration of Cargo: Here is a list I dictate to the students so that they are aware of all the different kinds of cargo taken on the ships that transported *les filles du roi* to the "New World." Having the students record the names of items prompts them to think actively about the items.

passengers	books
convicts	paper
sailors	spices
sheep	flour
cattle	oil
chickens	wine
straw	passengers' rations: sea biscuits, lard, beans, dried cod, and herring
mail	
cannonballs	
religious supplies (e.g., crucifixes, rosaries)	olive oil
	butter
bolts of cloth	mustard
wooden furniture	vinegar
dishes	fresh water
tools	cider

I ask the students to talk about how each of these items would be used and to generate questions. For instance, students often ask: How long was the journey? How would they keep the water fresh for months? How would they keep the food from going bad? Who would ration the food? Do you think that the sailors received more food than the women? What would happen if a baby was born during the journey? What was more precious — the cargo or the women? Were the women *considered* cargo? What value did they have? What happened if someone died on the journey?

Soundscape of a Ship's Hold: For a music-related exercise, students work in small groups imagining the interior hold of a French ship in response to hearing the text that follows. They then experiment with different ways to create that environment through sounds, perhaps using voice, body percussion, found objects, and simple instruments. They improvise and experiment with volume, pace, tone, tempo, repetition, emotion, and timing to find the most effective combination of sounds that will represent the environment. Each group of students or the teacher orchestrates the soundscape as other students listen.

Next, I read the following text aloud and then hand out copies of it to each small group.

This text is based on www.angelfire.com/ma3/noelofbrockton/page36.html.

> Travel by sea in the 1600s was a long, primitive, and difficult undertaking. There were no private rooms or even cubicles for the passengers; they traveled in the ship's hold.
>
> There were also the food animals — live chickens, pigs, cows — that were brought along to be slaughtered as needed for meals during the journey.

These conditions were tolerable if the weather permitted one to stroll about the deck and breathe the fresh ocean air. But if the weather turned mean, passengers were confined to the hold — with the weather shut out and unable to vent the odors of human waste and livestock.

This was also a breeding ground for all manner of bacteria. The passengers frequently suffered with boils, fever, and dysentery.

They also suffered from scurvy due to the limited diet that was provided. One estimate claims that about 10 percent of the *filles du roi* died at sea.

Bad storms and pirates were also a concern during the crossing.

Know, Infer, Inquire: *What do we know? What do we infer? What do we want to know? Who can tell us?* The premise of this exercise is that ideas flow from good questions, and good questions flow from bright ideas. Questions lead to further questions, and critical thinking becomes the root of good teaching. Students have applied the four questions (see page 106), as part of the unit.

The text featured below invites students to think about what they know, infer, and want to know about the topic, and who might be able to tell them more. Although derived from history, the diary excerpt is fictitious, but it is interesting to note that many of *les filles du roi* were literate, unlike most of the men they came to marry. An outline of how to pursue their inquiry follows.

> **Unanswered Questions: Excerpt from the Diary of Sophie Leduc, April 1664**
>
> Marie LaFontaine has disappeared! Georges reported her missing at 2 o'clock on Sunday afternoon. He entered my kitchen like a madman. He, Claude and about five other men from the village scoured the woods and fields until the pelting rain and sleet sent them inside around midnight. Marie is nowhere to be found.
>
> She did not come to Church that morning. When I asked Georges about her, he said that she had felt unwell. Apparently, when he returned from Church, his lunch was on the table. It was still hot. The floors had been swept and everything seemed in order. There was even a jar of snowdrops — freshly picked — in the centre of the table. When Georges called for Marie, there was no answer. The house was empty. Then he came to us for help.
>
> I cannot believe that this has happened. Marie was so beautiful — unforgettable, really. She came from Saint-Thomas-de-Touques in Normandy. She was an orphan but somehow had a dowry of goods valued at 300 livres. She was the first of the les filles du roi to be married. Her wedding was just over four months ago. She seemed so happy …
>
> Some people say that Marie has a fiery disposition and an independent spirit, but it was she who kept our dreams alive on that dreadful journey over the ocean from France. She was determined to survive the indignities of the ship — the sickness, the weather, the sailors. It was she who helped us all to have courage.
>
> Oh, Marie! Where are you? What has happened?

Sidebar: As students address the questions, encourage them to pay attention to details, imagine different scenarios, keep their minds open to possibilities, and search for hidden clues and subtexts to the information they are working with. As they become involved in tasks that encourage them to go beyond factual recall, they might discover underlying assumptions and hidden intent. They become critical thinkers who realize that the world is full of ambiguities. Their task as learners, then, is to constantly sift through facts, perceptions, memories, and theories, and play with ideas so that they are better aware of the world's complexity.

1. Ask the students to get into small groups. Hand each group a copy of the line master "Knowledge, Inference, Inquiry," found on page 106. (Or, you could have them copy the chart onto flipchart paper to make it easier to collaborate.) Ask them to appoint a recorder.
2. Have the groups brainstorm everything they know for sure about Marie LaFontaine. They are to write these facts down and identify the lines from the diary excerpt that gave them that information, in the far-left column of their chart.
3. In the next column over, the students record what they have inferred about the relationships Marie had with various people, her personality, her character, her history, and so on, along with the specific line in the diary text that drew them to that conclusion.
4. Prompt the students to record all their questions about Marie and Georges in the next column. For example, they might write: Was Marie a lot younger than her husband? Were there tensions in the relationship? Why might those tensions exist? Ask them think about Marie's "fiery disposition." How could her personality have caused problems in the community or with the church? What happened on the voyage over? What was it that Marie did to help the weaker women survive? What stories are told about her in the community? Did she fit in, or was she considered a rebel?
5. To complete the line master, have the students brainstorm a list of artifacts or people other than Marie herself who might be able to answer these questions. Candidates likely include the priest, Sophie, a neighbor, and the captain of the ship that brought *les filles du roi* to New France.
6. Ask for a volunteer from each small group to play one of the characters identified. Arrange the whole class in a circle, and invite one person in role at a time to answer questions. Students invent more as they improvise. They do not plan or prepare their responses. They live in the moment and react to each other's ideas. The whole thing can become quite powerful, and students are often riveted by the unfolding story. Having five or six students in role works well.
7. Once all the interviews with characters who might know something about Marie are finished, ask the whole class these questions:
   - What questions are still unanswered?
   - Why is it important to know the answers to these questions?
   - What has been revealed about *les filles du roi*, New France, the role of the Roman Catholic Church, and the life of the habitants that piques your interest even more?
   - What other aspect of New France would you like to explore and why?

"The purpose of art is to lay bare the questions that have been hidden by the answers."
— James Baldwin

The history and drama dynamic

This kind of improvisational work is layered like a tapestry. One works from what the students want to know, and the individual threads from the subjects and disciplines are woven together artistically to give students an experience of history, language, visual arts, music, drama, and geography. The tapestry cannot exist without the belief that students can imagine other realities and become involved in re-creating historical lives with purpose and intensity.

Creative expression through drama can act as a rehearsal space for real understanding of how history played out in individual lives. Cecily O'Neill reminds us that history is about *authenticated* realities and that drama is about *imagined* realities. Having the two threads intertwine in this curriculum tapestry provides an experience for students that informs their understanding of the facts and takes them into both intellectual and emotional realms, where they empathize with the women and gain different perspectives, allowing them to think about history in new ways.

Models of Innovative and Integrated Inquiry Projects

In "Education: The Case for Making It Personal," Ron Wolk (2010) describes the "personalized school" as a place where learners' voices are encouraged and heard. Students play a significant role in designing their own curriculum, which usually emphasizes real-world learning. Teachers become facilitators who guide students in educating themselves, tutor them, aid in finding resources, have them gain new understandings through innovative teaching strategies, and help them manage their time and energy. Student learning is assessed on the basis of actual work as shown in portfolios, exhibitions, special projects and presentations, experiments, recitals, performances, and demonstrations.

Innovative classrooms provide models of active interaction, where there are multiple levels of human experience and expression. Students are engaged in cognitive, aesthetic, emotional, physical (hands-on, body), social, and spiritual learning. There is individual and shared inquiry. There is a focus on the importance of metacognitive reflection, where students not only talk and write about what they are exploring, but also have opportunities to artistically represent their learning.

As noted earlier, since September 2014, I have served as the principal investigator for a large-scale Ontario Ministry of Education research project. *All I's on Education: Imagination, Integration, Innovation* has been taking place in 10 school boards with representation from the French, English, public, and Catholic sectors. It includes participants from elementary, secondary, urban, suburban, and rural schools, as well as First Nations, Métis, and Inuit students. The project was developed through the Council of Ontario Directors of Education (CODE) and funded by the Ontario Ministry of Education. The research focus has been on developing new conversations about how the teaching and learning in math, science, and the arts can be enhanced by inventive, integrated pedagogy supported by technology. Teachers and students have worked artistically with common concepts, contexts, ideas, themes, issues, and relationships found in and across various subjects.

As part of the project, my York University Faculty of Education research team and I spent 52 days working in 10 Ontario schools with 30 teachers and about 900 students from across the province. We made several visits to each school to support the teachers in planning and implementing innovative and integrated inquiry projects. These 10 inquiry projects are connected to students' interests, identities, and realities. They also align with the curriculum expectations of the provincial ministry of education.

I have outlined the *All I's on Education* projects as models of innovative and integrated inquiry projects, drawing on the power of the arts, to help you appreciate the potential of such projects and gain a sense of how each project is uniquely appropriate to its context.

Ten inquiry project summaries

Bluewater District School Board
Macphail Memorial Elementary School

Conseil Scolaire Viamonde
École Élémentaire La Fontaine

Dufferin-Peel Catholic District School Board
St. Cornelius Catholic Elementary School

Greater Essex County District School Board
General Brock Public School

Halton District School Board
Irma Coulson Public School

Lakehead District School Board
Armstrong Public School

Toronto Catholic District School Board
Madonna Catholic Secondary School

Artists from the school communities represented in the *All I's on Education* project joined the inquiry projects. Along with the teachers, students, and researchers, they collaboratively invented new approaches to curriculum.

Grey Matter: French immersion students in Grades 4, 5, 7, and 8 at Macphail Memorial Elementary School in Flesherton worked in music, dance, drama, science, math, and social studies to explore how change affects a community. Students improvised and presented scenes in a musical performance, raising awareness about the past, present, and future of Grey County.

Seeing with New Eyes: Students in Grades 4 and 5 at Ecole Élémentaire La Fontaine in Kleinburg engaged in drama by adopting the role of scientists to conduct research into the effects of the extraction of minerals on the human and natural environment. Grade 1 students, in role as inventors, conferred with the older students as scientists and responded to their questions in a final *collective drama* that drew on the students' knowledge in math, science, and visual arts. Students had opportunities to debate ideas and critique inventions.

Imagine a Place, Imagine a Time: Students in Grades 2 and 4 at St. Cornelius Catholic Elementary School in Caledon East ignited their imaginations in math, science, drama, music, visual arts, and technology. The Grade 2 class identified how the appearance and disappearance of snow has an impact on their lives, shapes their community, and develops their identities as Canadians. The Grade 4 class explored the appearance and disappearance of inventions while taking an imaginary time-machine journey to ancient civilizations.

Looking at the Over-Looked: Students in Grades 3, 5, and 6 at General Brock Public School in Windsor went on a series of community walks in and around historically significant "Olde Sandwich Towne" to record people, places, and artifacts that have, for a variety of reasons, been "the over-looked." After the students discovered various "hidden gems," such as forgotten historic buildings, in their community, they created *mediaographies* (see page 100) that tell the stories of appearance and disappearance through math, technology, science, and the arts.

Stand in the Place Where You Live: Students in Grades 7 and 8 at Irma Coulson Public School in Milton worked in math, science, dramatic arts, visual arts, and technology to explore their connections to the place where they live and learn. Through a series of activities, they radiated out of their center, literally and figuratively, to discover what makes a community live harmoniously. Their investigations culminated in a *collective drama* in which they articulated their connection to the land, the water, their past, their present, and their future lives.

Lost, But Not Forgotten: Students in Junior and Senior Kindergarten and in Grades 4, 7, and 8 at Armstrong Public School worked in math, science, technology, and visual arts to explore the stories of their community, including those of an abandoned town on the outskirts of Armstrong. Students worked with maps, still photographs, and oral histories to examine the human and environmental pressures that created change. They represented their understanding of what happened to the abandoned structures in a series of *photo-essays* that were placed on display at a community event.

Shining a Light on School Stigmas: Students in the Leadership Club at Madonna Catholic Secondary School worked in math and the arts to investigate the impact of stigmatization on student mental health. They drew maps of the areas in the school that were connected to their personal and collective identities, and using that information, choreographed a *dance* that was performed at Camp Olympia in front of an audience of other student leaders from across the Toronto Catholic District School Board.

Toronto District School Board
Runnymede Collegiate Institute

Trillium Lakelands District School Board
Archie Stouffer Elementary School

Windsor-Essex Catholic District School Board
St. Pius X Catholic Elementary School

Time Is Precious: Students in the Grade 9 Stell@r and visual arts programs at Runnymede Collegiate Institute worked in science, technology, and visual arts to create provocative *stop-time animation documentaries,* allowing them to explore the idea of what is worth preserving in their past, present, and future worlds.

Into the Woods: Students in Grades 2, 3, 7, and 8 at Archie Stouffer Elementary School conducted a micro-study of areas in the forest around their school in Minden. Students engaged in math, science, technology, and the arts, using iPads to capture their investigations in the forest through videography and still images. They created a series of *video postcards* that represented their understanding of the ecological and aesthetic significance of the forest to themselves and their community (see the text box below).

Planting the Seeds of Proportional Reasoning: Students in Grades 3, 4, 5, and 7 at St. Pius X in Windsor worked with scale, equivalence, and proportional reasoning in math, technology, and visual arts to re-create aspects of a beloved outdoor classroom. Students used mathematical reasoning to create *wind chimes* and *mosaics,* hanging the wind chimes and setting their stone mosaics into the ground of what became a most attractive and effective outdoor learning space.

Learning Brought Home: Real Reasons to Speak

As part of "Into the Woods," described above, I worked in Archie Stouffer Elementary School, which was surrounded by acres of woodland that belonged to the school. In the project the teachers developed, the students became stewards of that great forest and learned how to appreciate its beauty, purpose, design, and future. The project, being fully integrated, spanned a theme *and* went within and across subjects. The work was developmentally appropriate, socially engaging for the students, motivating, and relevant to their lives.

In one related drama experience, the students went in role as people whose livelihood depended on the forest and met a developer (a teacher in role) who wanted to destroy the old to make way for the new. The pressure for the students to speak in role was authentic, and they spoke poetically and powerfully as they advocated for the beauty of the forest to be left undiminished by corporate expansion. Here is one student's strong response:

> I'm done. I live in this forest. It provides me with a life. Because of it I can eat. You can't take my home away from me. I can't pay for a new home. Don't you get it? Here — here are a lot more photographs you can look at so that you might begin to understand.

The students used the photographs that they had taken of the various parts of the forest to defend its beauty and its importance to their lives. One student talked about how "ebullient" the forest was and argued for its preservation.

In this drama I was able to see how the making of art (photography) armed the students with material that they could use in their scientific inquiries into environmental preservation. They also used art to defend the science of the balance of nature and spoke in role with emotion and clarity. This experience was truly integrative for me (as teacher) and for the students, as well.

Culminating Events for Integrated Units

"Not everything that matters can be measured, and not everything that can be measured matters."
— Elliott Eisner

At the end of any integrated unit is a culminating event, perhaps a summative assessment tool. Your class may be able to share its creative results with another class, with the other classes in your division, with students in a higher or lower grade, or even with the whole school. In the section below, three kinds of culminating events are outlined: an anthology presentation, mediaographies, and a Gallery Walk.

An anthology presentation

An anthology is a performance of different kinds of material that is organized and delivered in a provocative way. Here are the initial directions I give:

"Decide upon an interesting topic. This topic must be agreed upon by all members of the group. Your task is to illustrate this topic using three poems, three pieces of prose, and the words and/or music of one song. The material should be put together in an interesting and unique way so that the message to the audience is clear and the theatre experience is unique. In other words, you are required to stage the material in the most dramatically effective way possible."

In their small groups, students can collect material for their anthology project from articles, statistics, historical documents, photographs, paintings, and pictures, and excerpts from short stories, play scripts, poetry, music lyrics, or novels.

Each group can consider any of the following presentation options in the staging of the anthology: (1) tableaux, (2) Readers Theatre, (3) choreography, (4) monologue, and (5) technology enhancements.

The way members write a script is to improvise from the source. They should get up on their feet as soon as they have collected the required number of sources and experiment with all the ideas presented. It is important not to reject somebody's idea until the group has done some work on it. Members should strive to ensure that transitions between each scene are smooth and that the beginning and ending of the anthology are effective.

The end result of each group's labor will be a well-rehearsed, structurally unified dramatic presentation of 10 minutes duration.

Here, the process generally used in creating an anthology presentation is shown as steps:

1. Each small group decides on the theme that they wish to explore dramatically. This theme can be general, such as hate or love, or specific, such as why people fight. If the theme is general, it usually becomes more specific as the group decides which aspects of the theme they are most interested in. It is important to remember that choosing a theme is extremely difficult and should involve full discussion by all members of the group. There is no point in trying to create something to which everyone is not committed.
2. After the theme is chosen, each group member is responsible for finding and bringing in material that relates to the theme in some significant way. Remember that this material can be drawn from a wide range of sources.
3. The group next examines, discusses, and analyzes the material found, retaining those things that it considers dramatically effective and setting aside anything that does not fit the theme or will be difficult to represent. Choice of material will depend on the length of the anthology.

Finding Affirmation in Group Work
Karina, one of my students who took part in building an anthology in a small group, wrote this in her evaluation:

"I learned that art activities are not restricted to 'art gifted' students. In our presentation, everybody had a part to do — whether it was acting, playing an instrument, providing the ideas, or critically assessing the performance. Projects like this anthology are a great way to bring everyone together where every person felt valued and appreciated. Speaking about my own experience with the anthology presentation, I really felt needed and valued, which helped me to come up with creative ideas and thoughts. Thus, I realized that in order to foster creativity in my own students, the first thing to consider should be establishing the environment, which is safe and positive. . . .

"I learned to never underestimate myself. We all have a habit of getting used to ourselves. And when we worked in groups, it was a great opportunity for me to rediscover myself through feedback of my colleagues. What seemed like an ordinary thing at first (for instance, playing a flute) can really enrich and add colors to any project or lesson."

4. After selecting the material, the group decides on the order in which the material will be presented. Particular attention should be paid to a strong beginning and ending for the anthology.
5. The group begins to work with pieces of material. It is not necessary to work through the selections from beginning to end at this point; rather, it is important to start interpreting the selections dramatically.
6. The next major problem is linking one selection to the next. Transitions are important because they provide continuity. Since there will not be a plot or any main characters, the focus is on the anthology showing aspects of the theme in a way that is logical or dramatically powerful. Transitions can be effectively created through movement, song, recurring statements, improvisation, or any other means that will take the audience from one scene into the next.
7. At this point in rehearsal, some material may not be satisfactory and will have to be changed. Students may want to rearrange some material, which is perfectly normal in the creative process, and analysis and discussion of these matters should be encouraged. Remind students that they are involved in a group creative process and that the perceptions of others are invaluable in helping to make the presentation the best it can be.
8. When the order of the selections has been agreed upon, pieces have been rehearsed, and transitions have been established, it is time to work on the beginning and ending of the presentation. Advise students that an effective beginning states the theme in some way and draws the audience into the presentation, and the ending is a final statement of the group's thoughts and feelings about the theme, which should leave the audience thinking about the presentation and its ideas.

Mediaographies

A mediagraphy is a collection of media pieces such as film, music, and audio clips presented in a video with voice-over commentary provided. Students work in small groups, choosing the media to be presented and the sequence that will work artistically.

While researching the Acadian Expulsion (see the unit outlined on pages 83 to 87), I discovered that many of the Acadians' personal objects were just left on the beach — they never made it onto the ships and were discarded. When the new British settlers arrived in the same location a few years later, they found these objects, including candlesticks, pottery, and linens, still there.

So, an appropriate culminating task could be to have the students tell the story of these forgotten objects through different media, such as photography, video, writing, filmed monologues, voice-over, and soundscapes. They could each create a *mediaography*, something that tells a story about a place, an object, or a person or persons of significance through a variety of media. They could create the objects in different ways, draw or paint them, find real objects and "antique" them, create a collage of them, and write a short history of their significance.

The classroom could become a place where these objects are presented in some significant way. Have students decide how to place them on a table, in a bookcase, or in some other place. Prompt them to consider and address these ideas: "What objects should be grouped together and why? What should be highlighted? How will the narrative of each object be represented? Could a video of voices accompany the display? Could there be created a background soundscape of wailing as when the men, women, and children were separated and forced onto different ships?" In this context, creating mediagraphies could allow students to bring to life the forgotten history of the Acadian Expulsion in a contemporary classroom.

The Gallery Walk

One event that works well as a culminating event is a Gallery Walk, which is often developed by several teachers. You and your colleagues could create a plan as you decide how the gallery will work: Where will the exhibits be located? How will students move from exhibit to exhibit? What time will be given to students to talk about their responses with other students?

A Gallery Walk is similar to visiting an art gallery or a museum. Students visit other students/artists, interact with their creations and discoveries, and ask questions to learn about different art forms and a variety of media. They can spend time moving about the gallery, sitting and watching special events, and viewing screens and displays on the walls. Students see multiple approaches to different ideas and ways of using the different art forms to make emotional and intellectual meanings.

Because students support the ideas of others and reflect on their own artistic progress, the gallery can be considered almost a team-building activity. Some of the exhibits might begin with the same resource. Some might be created by students in different grades. Others will be about related topics.

In a Gallery Walk, students may have opportunities
- to view student art on the walls, crafts on tables, and images on screens
- to listen to songs and music composed or played and sung by students
- to watch scenes developed from drama situations
- to hear poems and stories told and read aloud
- to see students in tableaux or sharing ideas through moving and dancing
- to observe on-screen compositions — videos, photographs, mixed-media constructions

Gallery Walks are important ways for your students to see how different ideas can be represented artistically. You might want to have each of your students carry a small notebook for listing questions, recording responses, and noting new ideas for another artistic project. A graphic organizer can help them keep track of their observations. The students can respond in an interview situation on videotape or record their responses in writing. The outline of a simple graphic organizer appears below.

Gallery Walk

Name of the gallery:
What caught your eye?
Describe the item:
What impressed you about it?
Why do you think that you were affected by it? (Did it remind you of anything? Did it disturb you in any way? Did it make you wonder about something else?)
What questions do you have for the artist(s)?
How did the overall impression of the gallery affect you?
What would you change, and how would you change it?

Because these galleries are interactive, students are encouraged to compare their responses with those of other students, to seek to understand the ideas of others, and to gain and give feedback. After participating in a Gallery Walk, students spend time with their classmates discussing different responses, noticing the variety of media and modes used by different students, addressing questions that arose, and collecting ideas for use in further lessons.

In this way, galleries are powerful summative assessment tools to allow students to reflect on their learning experiences.

A Checklist for Achievement

As teachers co-plan the inquiry project, determine activities, and map out the strategies that they will use, they may decide to use this checklist to help ensure that they are meeting the standards of achievement:

Engagement:
☐ Do the activities we have planned support the final culminating task?
☐ Have we designed an initial activity that will not only intrigue students but propel them into wanting to know more?
☐ Have we looked carefully at our students' diverse learning needs? How will we build in smaller, supported interventions for the students who need them, so that, in the end, all our students are successful?
☐ Once we begin to talk to students about the topic, let's find out the answers to these questions: What do they already know? What questions do they have? What myths or misconceptions do they have?

Co-construction of Knowledge and Understanding:
Let's have a plan on how to steer students to new understandings.
☐ How do we co-establish what quality work will look like? What kind of rubric or exemplar will we co-create with our students to establish criteria for excellent work? How can students see work by both adults and other students that will help them understand the essential standards of the work they are undertaking?
☐ Have we allowed for time to plan effectively? Are we flexible enough to continue designing activities as the task unfolds? How and when will we check in regularly with each other to see if we need to revise specific lessons?
☐ Have we given our students choice?
☐ What resources do we have at our disposal? Are there other artists, field trips (including virtual field trips), Internet sites, stories, and videos that we could draw on? Have we gathered enough ideas from our colleagues and tapped into the resources in our community?
☐ Is the student work designed to address and help answer the original inquiry question? Does it lead to greater understanding?

Assessment and Evaluation:
☐ At what points in the project should a student be able to describe what he or she is learning?
☐ What forms could these learning descriptions take?
☐ How can these descriptions be turned into an ongoing learning road map for the whole class?
☐ Why and how should the project be published, exhibited, or performed?
☐ How can we share the project with the larger school and artistic communities and beyond?

A Team Approach to Curriculum Integration

Integrating themes and topics, within and across subjects, are some ways that teachers can conquer a crowded curriculum. Teachers can look for and then take up the threads in the very busy tapestry called the curriculum. Sometimes, the threads mesh together beautifully, and the final product works. At other times, threads need to be dropped if the whole thing seems forced and unworthy of the work that should be done.

One underlying aspect of this work is the desire to do something different, to shake things up a bit, to take risks, and to begin a journey with various destinations in mind. It takes a certain kind of teacher to do this — one with the confidence to take some risks while trying something new. It also takes a team approach so that when the work gets too complicated, there are various eyes on the project. There is honest feedback, good advice, critical understandings about the purpose of the work, and encouragement to take learning to new heights and keep going. The knowing eyes of teachers will encourage a kind of reflection that can permit a change in direction, abandonment of certain aspects of the project that might not be working, and help in pursuing other goals.

A great thing about working this way is that the students are co-developers of the learning. Their input, imagination, and innovative thinking will have an impact on the outcomes of every project. Because the integrated classroom is a negotiated space open to disruption, risk, and new ideas, there needs to be a push-back against any kind of restraint. Nothing should be boxed in. Expectations should be flexible. The tapestry that is woven is dependent on improvisation, good will, hard work, and the imaginative capabilities of everyone involved.

Planning an Integrated Unit: Questions to Guide You

Consider what we know about our students.
- Let's think carefully about all the students we teach. What are the challenges?
- Have we considered all their learning styles and intelligences?
- How can we ensure that the students will enjoy the experience, find the ideas and concepts personally relevant, become engaged, and be motivated to ask questions to guide the project?

Address how to engage students in imaginative ways.
- What can we design to interest and challenge everyone?
- What can we design to allow students to become creative, critical, and independent learners?

Be sure to link integration to expectations.
- Let's think about what is expected in terms of standards and expectations.
- How many subjects can we integrate without forcing the connections?
- What theme or topic will be large enough and important enough for rich integration to take place?
- What kinds of human stories or stories about the world can we find to engage students?

Address time issues.
- What's feasible in terms of time?
- How can we restructure the schedule and timetable?
- How can we be sure to find the time to plan together?

Consider assessment and evaluation.
- What do we want students to know and be able to do by the end of this unit?
- How will we be able to measure their learning?
- What kinds of performance tasks will inform us of all this learning?
- How can we ensure that the judgments we are going to make are fair?
- What kind of culminating task can we design to inspire the students to keep working towards a learning goal that matters?
- Have we given thought to student ownership of the assessment process?
- Have we given voice and choice to students in terms of assessment?

Planning an Integrated Unit: Questions to Guide You (continued)

Establish resources.
- How can we set up this unit so that students do the research they need to do to make this work successful?
- What kinds of human stories can we find to engage the students?
- What kinds of artifacts can we bring into the classroom?
- Who in the community can we call on to be a guest speaker, artist in the classroom, or expert?
- What field trips can we organize to enhance what is being learned?
- How can we use technology to enhance learning?

Reflect on and refine the process.
- How can we organize ourselves to get feedback from staff, administration, and students so the learning experience can be enhanced?
- Where can we publish our results so that the work we have done can serve as a resource for others?

Knowledge, Inference, Inquiry

What do we know?	What do we infer?	What do we want to know?	Who can tell us?

5

With New and Open Eyes — Innovation

"The voyage of discovery is not in seeking new landscapes but in having new eyes."
— Marcel Proust

Our Real Work

... It may be that when we no longer know what to do,
we have come to our real work
and when we no longer know which way to go,
we have begun our real journey.

The mind that is not baffled is not employed.
The impeded stream is the one that sings.
— Wendell Berry, in *The Writer's Almanac* with Garrison Keillor

Innovation: Questions to Consider

How does creativity flourish in the classroom?
What insights about teaching and learning arise from multiplicity and ambiguity?

How do you keep going? How do you make every day fresh, keep your ideas from going stale? How do you create learning environments that are rigorous, responsive, inclusive, artistic, and exciting? How do you prevent yourself from feeling overwhelmed or discouraged because of the complications and circumstances of your teaching situation? How do you become aware of your own pedagogical signature and teaching identities and be open to including new ideas in your teaching repertoire? How do you push yourself out of your comfort zone, take risks, and try new ways of teaching? These questions haunt all of us who want to make a difference in the lives of our students.

And we might also ask ourselves other questions as we continue to teach year after year. For example:

- How can I improve the quality of the language I use in the classroom so that it is evocative, intentional, and beautiful?
- How can I improve my questioning to make it both rigorous and flexible?
- How can I ensure that I elicit remarkable levels of commitment to learning from my students?
- How can I extend my skills and reflect on my practice so that my teaching repertoire is constantly changing and expanding?
- How can I interrupt and disrupt the classroom experience by providing new information and new teaching methodologies so that I challenge my students' thinking and ways of knowing?
- How can I pull aside the curtains of doubt and seek out alternative, more imaginative ways to teach?
- How can I keep the conversation about the work alive with my colleagues so that we find ways to support and challenge one another in our innovative endeavors?

There are no easy answers to any of these questions.

So, ultimately, I can offer only what has worked for me.

Striving towards Moments of Significance

As a teacher, I am intent on giving my students a sense of the wider significance of what they are learning. I do this through questioning, the use of role-playing, the use of artifacts as props and prompts, the elevation of my language of instruction, and an understanding of how to use theatrical elements in my teaching. All of this emanates from a belief that there is an artistry to teaching and the aesthetics have the capacity to make the learning experience intriguing, compelling, and transformational.

Teaching to Transform Lives

"Some of us will struggle to defend what we love and work to make it contagious in our classrooms, even as we work for reflective awareness and for the kind of attending that may transform lives."
— Maxine Greene, *Variations on a Blue Guitar*, page 91

I find ways to engage students' attention right from the moment we encounter each other. I plan that encounter carefully. Once I have caught my students' attention, I encourage them to ask questions that have multiple answers. I use their questions as well as mine to activate the narrow, subject-based disciplines of the curriculum and move towards authentic, personal learning. I give my students activities to do individually or in small groups that help them work with the material they are learning. In this way they become actively involved — they talk, negotiate, problem-solve, argue, defend, create, rethink, make inferences, synthesize information, and connect what they thought they knew to what they are experiencing. At the end of each activity, I help them reflect on what they have learned and ask what more they need to know. In this way, I bring out in the open what my students already know but do not yet know that they know. Using my drama background, I work towards moments of significance and I don't settle for superficial response. I also make sure that I end the lesson in a way that makes my students want to come back and learn more.

Characteristics of Effective Teaching

Everyone approaches teaching differently, but we all want to ensure the success of our students. Here, I offer my kind of *pedagogical signature*, one approach to teaching that may prompt you to embrace something new.

Teachers need to be aware of their personal pedagogical signatures — what defines them as teachers and possibly as innovators. A pedagogical signature is linked to a tenet or belief that a teacher is known for: the teacher who is conscious of finding the value and worth in each child; the teacher who has the capacity to share stories that connect the curriculum to the real world both in the past and in the future, to his or her personal history, and to the way the world has unfolded over time; the teacher who gives solid context to the work; the teacher who uses sophisticated images, challenging quotations, diverse technology, music, and other things to inspire classroom conversations; the teacher who begins lessons with startling ideas and provocative questions that often start with "Did you ever wonder why . . . ?" or "What would happen if . . . ?" or "Let's suppose that . . ." Such a teacher is prepared not only in terms of knowledge but also in terms of imagination: the teacher, who depends on student response, has spent time imagining how the lesson is going to unfold and has multiple ideas of how to move the learning into deeper realms despite any roadblocks of behavior or misunderstandings. This teacher also demonstrates a willingness to stop and say, "This is not working" and will ask students for their input to move the learning along.

Components of One Pedagogical Signature

- A fascination about what can happen
- A desired uncertainty that is dependent on student response
- A willingness to improvise
- An awareness of all students' voices
- An appreciation of group process skills
- An openness to ambiguity and opportunity
- A readiness to consider all strategy options
- An insistence that student work be connected to real-world challenges
- A conscious choice to let students into one's teaching mind
- A sense of artistry
- A belief in students' potential

A fascination about what can happen

I need to be fascinated by what happens in schools and in classrooms. I am always interested in the kinds of relationships that are supported, the interactions that happen as a result, the way that the learning environment plays out, the teaching/learning dynamics, and the kind of classroom culture that is co-constructed by everyone involved. I never enter any classroom thinking that the experience of teaching and learning is going to be easy, but I do go in anticipating and wondering what will happen.

Through the years this fascination about learning and what lies ahead has kept me going. I walk into classrooms with a thoughtful plan, but I never know how it will play out for me or for my students. Lesson plans are simply maps, and curriculum gets "worked on" by the people who engage with it. All the time, I am conscious of context, interaction, and response.

A desired uncertainty that is dependent on student response

Just keeping that little frisson of excitement makes me happy and content. There has to be a certain pleasurable intensity to the work. Not knowing if a lesson is going to go as planned is, for me, the way I want it to be. The uncertainty makes me more responsive to the students. I am on edge. I listen more intensely. I think about what the students are saying and doing. I work harder as a result.

I like being open to surprise — to the child who speaks up for the first time about something that matters to her, to the child who finds it difficult to work in groups because everyone assumes that an inability to speak English means he has no ideas; to the students who struggle to read and write but are propelled into doing so because the topic interests and engages them. How can I support them in their desire to know about the content, be included in the group activities, and become literate? In my planning I have to think about these students. I need to "imagine forward" and have some ideas and resources at hand.

A willingness to improvise

Although most teachers believe that students need a structured routine — and some students do, even most of the time — I like to improvise and jumble things up. I want students to enter the classroom wondering what will happen that might be different but still as exciting as yesterday. I want students to be open to the wonder that learning presents them with. I believe that they will not be open, if everything is so planned that there is no room for improvisation, response, and imagination.

When I work with teachers, I encourage them to adopt a strong let's-wait-and-see approach as they plan integrated inquiry projects. They will often say things like: "We cannot possibly know how to move forward until we begin to work with the students. If this is true inquiry, we will have to wait to see what questions emerge from the students before we can plan further."

An awareness of all students' voices

I believe in striving to hear students' voices and seeking out those students who do not speak easily or with confidence. As I encourage collaboration and reflection, I know that I need to be aware of the silent voices in the classroom. I encourage oral language on many levels and insist on making each activity inclusive. I bear in mind six understandings that underpin oral language:

1. There needs to be a reason to speak.
2. We often shape our ideas at the point of utterance.
3. We talk ourselves into understanding.
4. Language is how thought is made.
5. We talk to understand as well as to be understood.
6. Engagement often comes before understanding.

Different Kinds of Talk Required
"Teachers must ensure that students are able to use talk freely for its full range of function. They should be familiar with exploratory talk, in which they can sift new thoughts, sort out their own position, and share feelings, memories and ideas: and be able to talk more formally in public, able to hold their own, participate in discussions, and put and sustain a point of view. This will include the ability to listen to what others are saying and understand why they are saying it."
— Mike Torbe and Peter Medway, *Language, Teaching and Learning: A Climate for Learning*, vol. 1, page 7

> **"Let my words turn into sparks."**
> For inspiration, read all of the Marge Piercy poem "The Birthday of the World" from *The Crooked Inheritance* (published in 2006 by Alfred A. Knopf in New York).

I use the nine talk frames, outlined in Chapter 3 (pages 51 to 53), to guide my thinking and planning. I understand that, when using the talk frames, students
- engage in thoughtful learning conversations about compelling ideas
- listen and exchange ideas with interest and respect
- grow in their own communicative competence and confidence
- develop the power of listening and discussing ideas with others
- talk their way into new understandings and engaging explorations

And I recognize that students can easily move from one kind of talk to another — for example, from social to collaborative — often using more than one register at a time.

An appreciation of group process skills

Students need to know how to work effectively in groups: how to share leadership and be responsible for the group tasks and group function. They also need to be able to troubleshoot and find ways of solving issues that get in the way of learning.

I find that learning group process skills is invaluable for students. They will use these skills and information throughout their lives. They will also begin to realize how important it is to be influential in a group and to experience the satisfaction that comes from contributing to successful task completion. Students need to be taught that the most satisfactory way to work in groups is to strive for a consensus so that most members can live with the decisions being made. To reach consensus, everyone must be able to voice an opinion and be heard. Everyone also must be willing to let go of some of what they want in order for decisions to be made. This process of working together to achieve a task can happen only if the group is aware of and monitors the roles that everyone needs to play.

As a teacher with an appreciation of group process, I constantly check in and find out how things are going as groups discuss the assignment before them. I am interested in the task, but also interested in how the students are functioning as group members.

An openness to ambiguity and opportunity

Innovative teachers, I believe, are open to new ways of thinking, and they encourage their students to represent their learning in different ways. They help their students think deeply, ask questions that may have multiple answers, and guide students into applying their new knowledge in innovative ways. This understanding points to the need to provide ideas for ways that students can represent their learning: to do so in projects that are exciting and artistic. I want students to create authentic work for an audience that is interested in what they are going to read, watch, hear, and experience.

> **Preparation for the Future**
> "People use foresight every day. Why not explicitly teach students to use their natural human instinct to anticipate, plan, and influence their own future and the future of their organizations and communities? What greater mission could we as teachers have than to really prepare students for the future!"
> — Peter C. Bishop and Andy Hines, *Teaching about the Future*, page xvii

Teachers benefit when they become more comfortable with ambiguity — when they appreciate that there does not need to be one set way of planning or implementing the curriculum. I believe that imagining forward — opening oneself up to different ways of approaching the material at hand and the class that awaits you — is a conscious act.

Teachers need to be able to seize the opportunities that lie before them. They also have to know how to deftly employ the various strategies in their teaching repertoires to move things forward. In fact, a teacher's capacity to call upon a number of different strategies and apply them in various situations is what leads to innovation and renewal. So, for me, keeping teaching fresh and exciting is dependent on what I know and how I know how to do it. It is also about researching and reading about what is happening in classrooms around the world: I follow well-known educators on Twitter, subscribe to educational journals, and attend workshops and seminars to feed my teaching spirit and mind.

I tell my teacher candidates to think of teaching as the making of a delicious soup. You need a good stock, but then you can experiment — add certain spices, change things up, introduce new ideas. In the same way, teachers are wise to begin with a map of what they plan to do, but as they work with students, they modify this plan. They change direction, try a different approach, configure the class in a new way, ask for help, stop and find out from their students what they are learning, and then improvise new directions. Teaching decisions depend upon the response, needs, and involvement of the students.

A readiness to consider all strategy options

Knowing when to draw on certain strategies makes me stretch myself. I try to make visible my thinking about where I want to go. I sketch out a plan on paper. I do not put anything in boxes because that act seems to shut my ideas down. I list all the strategies I can think of that might apply in the situation I am facing and then I plan a number of ways to go. I try not to anticipate too much, but am ready with various ideas and open to the possibilities that await me.

An insistence that student work be connected to real-world challenges

I push for the work to be connected to the students' lived experiences: in other words, I endeavor to ensure that it is authentic. I want the work we are doing to be connected to the challenges of the modern world, so the themes that I work with and the material that I introduce give students practice in making sound judgments in the face of uncertainty, coping with ambiguity, balancing the consequences of difficult decisions, and responding well to surprise.

I also want the conversations to be complex and the outcomes, artistic. In innovative classrooms, there will always be a structure and boundaries, but there is also the expectation of surprise, change, discovery, new ways of thinking, conversations about difficult knowledge, controversial issues — and more and more questions without solid answers.

In my teaching, I ask that students be conscious of the angles and locations from which they are viewing their worlds. I want them to be aware of how their perspectives have been shaped by personal experiences. Because everyone is different, disagreements and differing opinions in the classroom can be expected; however, I try to help students understand that what they are seeking is not one answer, but the means to keep looking for multiple answers to increasingly difficult questions. I feel successful if students can accept ambiguity and allow competing ideas and understandings to sit with them.

A conscious choice to let students into one's teaching mind

Over the years I have learned to tell students why I am structuring lessons in certain ways — I let students see into my teaching process. I ask my student

---

Risk versus Richness

"The improvised meal will be different from the planned one and certainly riskier, but rich with the possibility of delicious surprise."
— Mary Catherine Bateson, in *Composing a Life*, page 4

teachers: "How do you demystify what you are doing and what you are expecting?" I tell them it often helps to let students into their "teaching mind" — to give them an idea of what the goals of the exercise are, why they are structuring the classroom a certain way, what their expectations for student engagement and participation are, what the overall learning goals are, and how everyone is going to collectively achieve them.

A sense of artistry

I encourage teachers to pay attention to their presentation skills: to their use of expressive language. They are wise to consider how best to begin a lesson, how to read a story or poem out loud with dramatic emphasis, how to juxtapose various activities, scaffold lessons, and transition from one activity to another. Innovative teachers are aware of the presence of aesthetic form in their teaching — there is an artistry to what they do. They understand that the way in which they create learning opportunities is as important as the information itself. As Marshall McLuhan put it: "The medium is the message."

A belief in students' potential

Finally, I know I have to believe that all my students can become engaged in learning and achieve high standards. This imperative requires me to establish a strong work ethic and have high expectations, but it also means that I must provide lots of support for those who struggle and need encouragement.

Reflecting on teaching practice

I suggest using these questions to think about and reflect on how to help your students meet high expectations:
- What are my expectations for my students?
- How can I connect what they already know to what they want to know?
- What challenges can I set to pique their interest and keep them engaged?
- How can I encourage continuous improvement in every one of them?
- How am I taking responsibility for providing the variety of learning opportunities that each student needs to succeed?
- How can I differentiate my instruction by designing project-based inquiry that engages various students in different ways?
- How can I remain open to the voices of my students and commit to working with the questions that they create?
- How do I develop the capacity to really listen to what my students need and want to know?

What Effective Teachers Strive to Do

What I call the "6 Es of Effective Teaching" provide one way in which you can anchor your efforts to teach effectively and innovatively.

1. *Expect* much of all students, and provide them with lots of support to achieve those expectations.
2. *Establish* inclusive, culturally responsive, and respectful classrooms.

> 3. *Engage* learners in ways that help them become intrigued about the learning that lies ahead.
> 4. *Explore* material in inventive ways that honor all learning styles.
> 5. *Extend* the learning beyond superficial understandings.
> 6. *Evaluate* fairly. Evidence-based learning will foster fair assessment of the data that have been collected.
>
> This kind of teaching asks students and teachers to work with open eyes — to explore, learn new vocabulary that goes beyond labeling, consider different contexts, develop empathy, interpret qualities, imagine, and make connections.

Images of Dynamic Teaching: The 6 Rs

Dynamic Teaching: The 6 Rs
1. Reciprocity
2. Relationships
3. Respect
4. Risk
5. Resilience
6. Reflection

Teachers may benefit by thinking about themselves in relation to the "6 Rs" involved in teaching in imaginative, integrated ways: reciprocity, relationships, respect, risk, resilience, and reflection. The *reciprocity* that emanates from sharing our teaching stories is helpful and productive as well as comforting. Teachers need to help students *respect* themselves and others as well as the work that lies before them. They need to take *risks* and find *resilience* to cope with disappointments, turning to colleagues when things are not going as well as they could. They also need to *reflect* on what worked and what did not. Throughout their teaching, *relationships* are key.

1. Reciprocity — a glass of water

A story about a glass of water helped me think about teaching in a new way. I was invited to speak at a conference in Montréal and was delighted to be in my hometown working with arts educators from across North America. The keynote speaker, Michael Smith, introduced the conference. He played the piano and then spoke, telling stories of his work in schools and communities across the world.

One story stayed with me. Michael was invited to speak in a prison. He began (as he always does) by playing the piano as the audience members sat down. Out of the corner of his eye, he noticed a large man in the front row get up and leave the prison auditorium. Michael thought to himself, "Well, you can't win them all." He assumed that the man had left the space because he was not interested.

How to See Each Student

"A primary challenge to teachers is to see each student as a three-dimensional creature, a person much like themselves, with hopes, dreams, aspirations, skills and capacities; with a body and a mind and a heart and a spirit; with experience, history, a past, several possible pathways, a future. This knotty, complicated challenge requires patience, curiosity, wonder, awe, humility. It demands sustained focus, intelligent judgment, inquiry and investigation."
— William Ayers, *Teaching the Personal and the Political: Essays on Hope and Justice*, page 5

But a few minutes after Michael had made this judgment, the man reappeared with a glass of water, gently placed the glass on top of the piano, and said: "I thought you might need this. It is very dry in here." The man returned to his seat, and the performance began.

I tell that story in workshops to teachers because it reminds me that we have to be careful not to judge students by their initial behaviors. We need to metaphorically play the piano and wait to see who our students are and what they are all about. We need to defer judgment until we get to know them. For me, the glass of water is a symbol of reciprocity. Teaching is a two-way street, determined by a gentle kind of reciprocity. What the student receives, he often gives back. What the teacher gives, she often receives back in multiple ways.

113

> **The Character of Relationships**
>
> "The nature of relationships among the adults within a school has a greater influence on the character and quality of that school and on student accomplishment than anything else. If the relationships between administrators and teachers are trusting, generous, helpful, and cooperative, then the relationships between teachers and students, between students and students, and between teachers and parents are likely to be trusting, generous, helpful, and cooperative. If, on the other hand, relationships between administrators and teachers are fearful, competitive, suspicious, and corrosive, then these qualities will disseminate throughout the school community."
> — Roland S. Barth, in "Improving Relationships within the Schoolhouse," page 8

2. Relationships — a hospital clinic waiting room

When my husband was ill, I spent a lot of time waiting for him in the radiation clinic at Princess Margaret Hospital in Toronto. I used to watch the nurses and radiation technologists find the patients and then take them in for their treatment. There were a lot of very sick people: some were asleep, some were reading, others were holding hands with their loved ones. Some were just sitting quietly; others were talking with their families.

The nurses found their patient in different ways. If they were asleep, they gently woke them up. If they were reading, they carefully approached them and said hello. Some nurses joked with their patients and kidded them along; others just spoke quietly, unlocked their wheelchairs, and were off.

As a teacher, I watched these interactions with respect, wonder, and a bit of jealousy.

We ask teachers to establish relationships with students and differentiate the curriculum to meet their needs. But, unlike these nurses at Princess Margaret Hospital, teachers lack the luxury of a one-on-one relationship. They enter a full classroom and face a crowd of very different people, all of whom have to be attended to in different ways. The students' learning styles and particular needs and interests all have to be addressed.

I remind myself of this image when I speak to teachers about differentiating their instruction — and I am mindful of what a challenge it is to take into account all of the different kinds of relationships that exist in the classroom: the relationships of teachers to students, the relationships among the students, the relationships among the teachers, and the relationships to the curriculum: all key pieces in everyone's learning journey.

3. Respect — footsteps in the sand

In 2011 was invited to go to Paraguay by the Department of Foreign Affairs to speak on education and democracy. The group of Canadian academics with whom I travelled decided to visit the Iguazu Falls and hired a driver to take us. The man had lived in the United States and returned to Asunción to marry and have children. When his first child was born, he invited his niece to come into the city from the country to help his wife with the baby. The niece was 14 years old and had not gone to school; she therefore could not read.

After the first few days, the man gave his niece some money and asked her to go to the store to buy some milk and bread. She did not return. A search party was struck, and the girl was finally found. Her explanation was simple: She had lost her way. Her normal way of navigating the world in the village and its surroundings was to read her footsteps in the dirt or sand. Because the streets of Asunción were paved, she had lost her bearings and could not find her way home.

I love this story because it reminds me about the various ways that students "read" their world. As teachers, we have to find out about what they can do and how they do it, and then introduce them to other ways to navigate their future lives. We have to respect students' locations, and we have to help them respect each other. Just as important, we have to encourage them to respect the work that happens in the classroom and realize the importance of learning as an enterprise that can change their lives for the better.

> **Dialogue as a Way of Knowing**
>
> "We should respect the expectations that students have and the knowledge students have. Our tendency as teachers is to start from the point at which we are and not from the point at which the students are. The teacher has to be free to say to students, 'You convinced me.' Dialogue is not an empty instructional tactic, but a natural process of knowing."
> — Paulo Freire, in "Reading the Word, Reading the World," page 15

4. Risk — a bouquet of lilacs

In 2010, I was asked to facilitate a two-day seminar on ethical leadership at the Manitoba Association of School Superintendents in Gimli, Manitoba. The participants were the superintendents of the Manitoba district school boards — men and women who had to make difficult, ethical decisions every day.

I began by asking them to tell stories of the experiences that had shaped and propelled them into becoming educational leaders. The stories were moving, funny, and inspirational. One, in particular, stuck with me.

One superintendent said that he had been a high-school chemistry teacher. He was unsure of his teaching and managed to hook up with a group of teachers on the staff who were quite negative about everything. They said things like, "Just close your door and teach the way you want. These education reforms change all the time. Nobody will care." He taught the way that he had been taught and became cynical and negative early in his career.

Then he got married, and one beautiful June day his wife picked some lilacs, put them in a jar, and said, "Take these to school and put them in the staff room for everyone to enjoy." So he took the jar of lilacs to school and put them on a table in the center of the room.

As he was placing the lilacs on the table, one of his friends said to him: "What do you think this is? A funeral parlor?" The superintendent said that, at that point, he knew that he had to change — that he needed to move away from the negativity and begin to risk learning about teaching in new ways.

And he did, and this change made all the difference to him, to his students, and to his career.

I retell this story because it reminds me about how teachers can change if they take risks, move away from what is not working, and envision a new way of teaching and leading. This kind of risk taking can happen at any time in a teacher's career. To think in new ways and to discard old ways of doing things takes courage.

5. Resilience — Colette Bourgonje, Paralympic champion

Colette Bourgonje, a Paralympic cross-country skier and athlete, is an embodiment of resilience. Bourgonje won several medals in both the Summer and Winter Paralympics. Her silver medal at the 2010 Winter Paralympics was Canada's first medal at home.

Ever since a car accident in 1980 made her a paraplegic, Bourgonje has found life a struggle. The story of her recovery and triumph is heartbreaking, but it is also full of courage and resilience. It was a teacher who encouraged Bourgonje to follow her dreams after her accident and continue to be an extraordinary athlete.

I use the images of Bourgonje that were taken both before and after her accident to inspire teachers to keep going despite the challenges of teaching. Teaching requires dedication and commitment — the planning, the implementing to make it all work never lets up — and one must be prepared to give one's best and be innovative.

Ragged Teaching

"Much of teaching is tentative, contingent, and uncertain. We learn it by living it, by doing it, and so it is necessarily ragged and rough and unfinished. As with any journey, it can seem neat and certain, even painless, looking backward. On the road, looking forward, there is nothing easy or obvious about it. It is hard, grinding, difficult work. The collective, ongoing conversation about teaching allows us to glimpse something of the depth of this enterprise, to unearth the intellectual and ethical implications beneath the surface."
— William Ayers, *To Teach: The Journey of a Teacher*, page 1

> **Can Resilience Be Taught to Students?**
>
> There is a lot of discussion about teaching students "grit" and perseverance. Carol Dweck, a leading researcher on motivation, is influencing much of the thinking.
>
> Dweck highlights the factors that make a difference for all youth, but especially disadvantaged students. Schools can help students succeed by promoting, by design and via daily instruction, messages that tell students the following:
>
> - Your intelligence is something that can and will develop with effort, good strategies, and support from this school.
> - You have a purpose. You are "doing school" so that you can contribute something to your family and to the world.
> - You belong here, in this school — this school is for you.
> - We, as your teachers, will set high standards for you, and we will give you what you need to succeed.

6. Reflection — *an airplane taking off from the tarmac*

I was giving a presentation to the Saskatchewan Reading Council and was asked to sit at a table with a first-year teacher and a teacher who had been teaching for a long time. The three of us immediately hit it off as we began telling our teaching stories.

As the older teacher spoke, I knew that I was in the presence of someone special. She talked about the work that she had done in northern Saskatchewan in a First Nations community. She described the teaching encounters she had had and the kind of commitment that was needed to make a difference in the lives of the students. Both the first-year teacher and I were enthralled by her ideas, her passion, her insights, and her critical capacity to reflect on her teaching career.

The teacher also related a more personal side of her story. After she had been teaching in the community for a long time, her marriage came to an end. She decided she had to leave the community that she loved very much. She told the story of packing up and loading her own children into the small plane that was flying out.

There were many tearful farewells. Her students and their families, as well as the members of the band council, had come to say goodbye on the tarmac. As the plane took off, her son looked out the window and said, "Look, Mum." As the teacher looked out the window, she saw the entire community — children, parents, and others running down the tarmac — waving and begging her to stay.

I tell that story at the end of many workshops, encouraging teachers to reflect on their teaching and what impels them to stay in the profession. I say to my student teachers that, in the end, we want our students, their parents, and members of the community to metaphorically run down the tarmac, begging us to stay because of the impact our teaching and commitment to student learning has had on everyone.

Warmth for the Child's Soul

"One looks back with appreciation to the brilliant teachers, but with gratitude to those who touched our human feelings. The curriculum is so much necessary raw material, but warmth is the vital element for the growing plant and for the soul of the child."
— Carl Jung

Effects of Innovative Practice on Teachers

The Artistic Project of Teaching

"I keep reminding people (myself, as well as some of you) that teachers have their own crafts, their own repertoires, their own modes of artistry, even though they cannot call themselves practicing artists. But like the choreographers and directors and musicians and visual artists you work with here, you also have a life project, a way of being in the world through which and by means of which you define yourself as a person. The project is teaching, and if you are like me, it is a lifelong quest, a lifelong project. Like the artists, we are always in process, always exploring our texts, our raw materials, always seeking ways of reaching others, and moving others to come alive, to think about their thinking, to create meanings, to transform their lived worlds."
— Maxine Greene, *Variations on a Blue Guitar*, page 70

On the *All I's on Education* project, I have watched teachers and the team grow in their understanding of how layered and complicated the work of inquiry is. It is very much like creating a tapestry with interweaving threads of identity, inquiry, integration, and imagination to produce work that is innovative. In the professional development workshops, the research team and I have sought to provide the teachers with fresh ideas and approaches. They, in turn, have researched new ways of representing their students' learning in and through the arts with the support of technology.

I have made the following discoveries about these 10 teams of innovative teachers, representative of all teachers engaging their students in integrated inquiry projects:

- *The teaching teams are each making connections.* They have a vibrant relationship with the curriculum, with their students, with one another, with the community, and with the place in which they teach.
- *Members of each team are collaborating with one another.* They seek out support for the work that lies ahead, ask one another questions, and then find out what is being done in other places to support the kind of work they want to do. They believe in mentoring each other and realize that doing so is time spent well on the journey to teach.
- *The teaching teams understand project-based learning and the kinds of threads to be woven together.* They have embraced those "darn curriculum" documents and now see them as catalysts for learning. They are committing themselves to learning about this kind of teaching for the long term.
- *They have a revised understanding of what teaching is all about.* They have moved beyond thinking that procedural learning, or the acquisition of skills or knowledge to perform tasks, is what matters. They have embraced conceptual learning, where students take a factual base and then hypothesize, extrapolate, and discover more. They are comfortable working imaginatively with big ideas.
- *They dream.* What's more, they do their dreaming with the permission of the principal and board administration. They trust their instincts and follow their students into labyrinths of learning. They notice things that they did not notice before and are highly sensitive to classroom dynamics.
- *They are committed to innovative teaching.* As they assess and evaluate the learning that is happening in the inquiry projects, they are honest about their struggle to remain innovative, but they are determined to stay the course.

Towards an awakening to new ways

Students need to learn how to respect one another, value different opinions, share common experiences, and work towards a critical understanding of complex relationships and ideas. To do this, they require many opportunities to speak and write about what they are learning. They must connect the material before them to their lived experiences. We know that our students need lots of time to talk in the classroom so that they can find out about one another, imagine scenarios, share ideas about what they are learning, ask critical questions, negotiate meaning, gain new perspectives, analyze unforeseen circumstances, reflect on new knowledge, and talk themselves into understanding.

Classrooms, therefore, need to be places where students and their teachers are awakened to new ways of thinking and living in the world — where students and their teachers see, hear, and feel often in unexpected ways. Students need to be actively engaged in the material being presented so that they can construct meaning about what they are learning. Curriculum needs to be relevant, open-ended, integrated, and challenging. It has to matter.

After the teachers had completed the inquiry projects for the *All I's on Education* project, I asked them to respond to questions, these among them.

- How easy or difficult was it to collaborate with your colleagues to design innovative curriculum? Describe the process of pushing your teaching beyond what you already knew into what you wanted to know.
- What new awareness do you have about the role that innovation and integration can play in the teaching/learning dynamic? Please describe a significant moment in the project where you began to see teaching and learning in a new light.
- How did the process of representing your participation artistically shape your view of the project?
- What has been the most significant change in your practice since you began to teach this way?
- How did the teaching of the inquiry fit into your teaching schedule? Why?
- What has been the impact of innovative methodologies and practices on your experience as a teacher?

I invite you to consider these questions, too, as you work towards a more integrated approach to your teaching.

"Amazed, awed, humbled, inspired, moved"

"... In just one school day I experienced, felt, heard, and saw very 'big ideas' at work — the passage of time, the tyranny of hierarchical systems, young people's sense of identity and community, emotional intelligence, and gender politics to name but a few. And all connected to the actual Ontario Curriculum for Arts, Math, Sciences and Social Sciences! . . .

"Most importantly, the students involved reminded me that the most impactful and memorable moments in education come from the heart, from feeling safe to ask difficult questions, and from our own stories. I feel that our amazing kids really pondered, in meaningful and rich ways, who they are, where they live and where they come from today.

"I am more than a wee bit proud. Why can't every day at school be like this? . . ."
— Charlie Glasspool, Macphail Memorial Elementary School

A Sense of Magnitude

Below is an email exchange between me and a teacher, Tyler Boyle, about finding a way to integrate math into social science.

Tyler Boyle:
In this [math] strand, students develop their understanding of number by learning about different ways of representing numbers and about the relationships among numbers. They learn how to count in various ways, developing a sense of magnitude.

Kathy Lundy:
I love that the curriculum asks us to help kids develop "a sense of magnitude." Wow. That is pretty powerful.

When I think about the trek to New France, I consider that this has a sense of magnitude to it. How many kilometres from France to New France? How fast could those ships travel? How long was the journey? How much was dependent on weather and wind? Who figured all this out? What kind of technology was used? Can we take a look at how these things worked (or didn't)?

What kinds of supplies did the travellers need for the journey? What else did they bring to the New World? How were these supplies loaded into the ship? How did everything fit into the ships?

And in terms of status... who was awarded accommodation that was okay and who were squished together like sardines?

What happened to the people of the First Nations when the Europeans arrived? How did smallpox infect the First Nations community? Let's look at those statistics and get a sense of the *magnitude* of the disaster.

The curriculum asks us to consider teaching data management, allowing students to "estimate, use descriptions and discoveries by scientists, and estimate health risks." How many people made it to the New World? How many started out and did not make it? How could we predict who might make it? What were the conditions that made it difficult etc?

There is lots to talk about. This is the kind of curriculum integration and implementation that I have waited a lifetime to do with teachers. I am so thrilled that you are on the journey with us and are able to consider the gems that we will explore with your kids!

See you Thursday. Can't wait!

Thirty Arts Strategies to Move Learning Forward

Garfield Gini-Newman is a professor at the Ontario Institute for Studies in Education and a specialist in critical thinking. He reminds us that the material we present and the method we use to present it can be either "brain compatible" or "brain antagonistic." Both the content and the pedagogy matter — and for a diverse group of students who have different learning needs and challenges, the wider the repertoire of strategies and materials we possess, the more successful we will be. I am always on the lookout for material that is interesting, thought provoking, and challenging, and I look for various genres — picture books, newspaper articles, blogs, young adult fiction including graphic novels, scripts, pamphlets, poetry, and visual images.

I try to vary the strategies and scaffold them carefully as the lesson proceeds. When I plan lessons I aim to challenge my students to think in new ways. I might want them to investigate the bias of a letter to the editor, model their problem-solving skills for younger students, experiment with a wide range of language by creating poetry in specific ways, use different language registers to consider how people thought in a given time period, find alternative endings to a movie or theatre script, or compare and contrast the way people react to new ideas that challenge the status quo. The way I get my students to do this kind of critical thinking will depend on their language development, their skill level, their ability to work in groups, their commitment to the task, and their readiness and willingness to engage in challenging material.

I need to plan, but I also need to adjust the plan as soon as I meet the group — "The map is not the territory," as Richard Courtney wrote in *Play, Drama and Thought*. My lesson plan might be right there in my hands, but I am usually

The Role of the Arts in the Curriculum

"One of the first things that works as the arts develop is a sense of relationship, that nothing stands alone... every aspect of the work affects every other aspect... the arts teach the ability to engage the imagination as a source of content... they are among the most powerful ways we become human, and that is reason enough to earn them a place in our schools."
— Elliot Eisner, *Christian Science Monitor* (30 January 1997)

aware that I might have to adjust or throw out my ideas to teach the way that the students need to be taught. Andy Hargreaves speaks about the "Julie Andrews," or these-are-a-few-of-my-favorite-things, curriculum. While important to have favorite things — material, approaches, strategies, assessment tasks — it is equally important to put them aside when you need to teach in a way more compatible with the needs of your students.

Here are 30 innovative ways of teaching, many of which owe their power to the arts.

1. Active, Collective Listening and Response

This strategy allows students to experience an informal, personal reaction to what they are hearing or reading. As students share their reactions with others, they gain an understanding of the complexity of the text, which is open to various interpretations.

Students listen to a reading or audio recording of a text and jot down ideas and questions that come to mind. They can also do this as they read a text silently. They are encouraged to underline words or phrases, and they might circle words they don't understand to research. Everyone's responses and ideas can be discussed in small or large groups.

Example: *Macbeth*, Act 1, Scene 3

I have given many workshops on the teaching of Shakespeare. At one workshop with Grade 8 students, I decided to use the scene from *Macbeth* where Macbeth meets the witches for the second time. This scene is full to bursting with paradoxical images, statements, and even characters.

I had the students to listen to an audio recording of the 35-line scene. We talked as a class about whether or not the witches are seriously evil or just mischief making. We listed the kinds of powers they seemed to possess.

I then played the audio recording again and asked the students to notice how the witches' conversation follows a different rhythm from that of other characters in the play. In the first part of the scene, the witches speak in rhyming couplets; then, when Banquo and Macbeth arrive, they switch to normal speech, that is, prose. I asked: "Why do you think Shakespeare changed the pattern in this way?"

Here are three of the responses:

> Maybe it was important to make these characters really different than the others so Shakespeare made them speak in rhyme or in prose and not in iambic pentameter.

> I think that Shakespeare wanted the audience to really hear what the witches had to say so he did not make their speech too lofty and [made it] more accessible to everyone.

> I don't think the witches should speak in an educated way. They need to be different than the kings and nobles — they kind of need to be "earthy."

2. Artist Trading Cards

Students create cards on 2 1/2 by 3 1/2 inch (64 mm by 89 mm) cardstock to represent their understanding of what they are studying. They can represent a place (real or fictional) or a person or character from literature or history. They can depict objects, landmarks, events, or even words. The cards might be created in response to an experience in class, after a field trip, or at the end of a unit or a novel study. Students can make many artist trading cards — miniature works of art — and then trade them with others in the class. They can also sort them into collections, make anthologies filled with them, and display them.

Example: A response to a multi-genre exhibition on climate change

A group of Grade 3 students visited the McMichael Canadian Art Collection in Kleinburg, Ontario, to view *Vanishing Ice: Alpine and Polar Landscape in Art, 1775–2012*. Their teachers were implementing an integrated unit on climate change and wanted the students to see the exhibition because of its unique interweaving of art, history, and science. The exhibition consisted of more than 70 works by 50 artists, writers, and naturalists from 12 countries. Immediately after the visit, the students each created two artist trading cards and traded one of them. The cards were put on display in the library and featured on parents' night.

3. Bird's-Eye View: Threefold Perspective

Students record what they see, wonder, and imagine is happening in an image. They then talk about their different interpretations with a partner, in small groups, or with the class. This strategy allows students to be objective, then reflective, and finally imaginative about what they are seeing and learning. It also allows students to find a voice not their own and to experience what a bird's-eye view is like.

Students examine a piece of art related to what they are studying and consider what it reveals about the characters and the situation or event depicted.

- First, they simply decode the picture: *I see* . . .
- They then have an opportunity to access their prior knowledge: *I remember* . . .
- Finally, they make inferences about the image: *I imagine* . . .

They also consider the context, the artist's purpose, and the artist's interpretation.

Example: "It was a perfect lift-off."

For years I have used the portfolio edition of *The Mysteries of Harris Burdick*, which consists of 14 poster-size drawings, to bring joy, interpretation, imagination, and wonderings into many of my workshops and lessons. When I used the poster "It was a perfect lift-off" in a Grade 2 classroom, I asked the students to work in groups to tell me what they saw, remembered, and wondered about. I then asked them to become the neighbors of the house that lifted off and to tell stories in role of what they remembered of the family that lived there and what looked suspicious in the days before the house disappeared. Finally, they were prompted to wonder what might have happened. I played the role of the police investigator, asking questions, pushing as hard as I could to build a story that was truly mysterious.

4. Brainstorming (and Beyond)

Brainstorming is an opportunity for students to share their wealth of knowledge and experience. Groups of five or six can work well with one student recording the ideas generated by the group over a set time. Brainstorming allows groups of students to generate a "pool" of ideas, examples, and questions without fear of criticism or editing. Later, groups will work with the material to explore a topic or idea in greater depth. They can expand on one another's ideas, ask questions, enter into debate about the worth of an idea, and suggest alternatives. Brainstorming is also an effective listening exercise because it requires students to "work off" each other's ideas. Everyone's voice is heard.

Procedure for successful brainstorming
1. Appoint a recorder, and make sure that the recorder has a writing device: a large sheet of paper, a Smart Board, or a computer. Make sure that everyone can see it.
2. Appoint a timer, and make sure that the timer has access to a clock or a watch.
3. Listen to the instructions from the teacher.
4. Brainstorm for the allotted time without editing or comment making.
5. Try not to interrupt!
6. Continue recording as long as the ideas flow, but stop when the timer tells you to.
7. Listen to further instructions.

Example: A Cadillac called "the Beast"

A Grade 9 class was investigating the theme of security. They explored how security has affected the way people travel and the way that famous people conduct their lives. When I worked with them, I presented them with an image of the Beast — U.S. President Barack Obama's 2008 Cadillac. Students worked in groups to brainstorm the security features to be found on the outside and the inside of the vehicle. Once they had done so, I shared with them the Internet list of features, which included pump action shotguns and tear gas cannons, a military-grade body, armor-plated doors, and an oxygen and firefighting system. The item I mentioned last was this: bottles of the president's blood in case a transfusion was needed.

And then I described a time of limited security measures. I told the story of how, when I was 12 years old, I heard on the radio that President John F. Kennedy had been killed while sitting in an open convertible, his wife, Jackie, by his side. But this was not the story that affected my students — it was my memory of watching Jackie Kennedy stand beside Lyndon Johnson being sworn in on Air Force One. She had insisted on wearing the pink Dior suit with her dead husband's bloodstains on it. She wanted the world to see what had happened to her, to her family, and to her country in the most graphic way possible. My emotional memory of this is what had the greatest impact on the students.

Emotional Connections
Many arts education researchers write about the importance that feelings play in learning, and I try to find places in my teaching where I can weave emotional connections into the curriculum tapestry. I often ask students to share their own memories, invite guest speakers into my classroom to tell stories relating to what we are learning, and relate personal anecdotes that are full of emotion. I know that students often remember these stories more than they do anything else.

5. Bursting the Bubble

This strategy allows students to use the attributes of graphic novels to explore meaning, character motivations, and different interpretations. Students look at a specific frame. They analyze each character's posture, facial expressions, physical relationship to others in the frame, and place in the landscape. They then work with a partner to "burst the bubble" in the frame, adding more lines to express what a character is thinking, feeling, and wondering about. The partners share their "bursted bubbles" with another group and present this new dialogue in a short scene to the class.

For many summers I have had the privilege of teaching hundreds of teachers from Jiangsu province in China. They come to Canada for eight weeks to take the York University course "Oral Language Development through Drama." They are at various levels of English learning, and they are wary, if not intimidated by the active nature of drama.

Example: An early scene from the wordless book *The Arrival* by Shaun Tan

I had been searching for source material that could help me introduce drama concepts in a way that would connect to their lives and not put too much pressure on them in terms of English language fluency. I found it when I discovered *The Arrival* by Shaun Tan, an immigration story told as a series of wordless images. A man leaves his wife and child in an impoverished town, seeking better prospects in an unknown country on the other side of a vast ocean. He eventually finds himself in a bewildering city, where he is helped by sympathetic strangers, each carrying their own unspoken stories of struggle and survival. I planned a lesson but after I had spent some time with the teachers, I realized that I needed to do some vocabulary development work with them in order to make the drama work successful and satisfying.

I showed the first picture of the book on an overhead and asked the students to take a good, long look at it. The image is that of a man and a woman with their hands joined together and tea things on the table in front of them.

Working in partners, they decided what one of the characters was thinking, what the other one was saying, and what the caption could be at the top. Each pair recorded the information on a cut-out speech bubble, a cut-out thought bubble, and a square, colored sticky note. They then created minimal scripts, with each partner reading aloud the man's thoughts or words or the woman's thoughts or words, and one reading the caption. Here are two examples of the work created:

Caption: The Time Has Come
Woman (thought bubble): I am going to miss him so much . . .
Man (speech bubble): Please remember to write as often as you can . . .

Caption: The Final Farewell
Man (thought bubble): She is strong and will be able to live on without me . . .
Woman (speech bubble): Your tea is growing cold . . .

6. *Choral Speaking*

Choral speaking involves experimentation, interpretation, and rehearsal of a piece of text, for example, a poem. The students discuss the meaning of the text and consider who might be speaking and to whom. They explore what challenging texts mean by reading them aloud in many different ways. In small groups, they experiment with tempo, tone, pace, repetition, volume, emotion, and different kinds of groupings, such as solo, duet, trio, and whole group. They focus their attention on words, language patterns, and punctuation. In the time spent on finding meaning and powerful dramatic effect, students revisit the text many times and read the words in a wide variety of ways. They help one another and share ideas. As for struggling readers, they gain confidence in oral language response and in reading out loud because they are blending their voices with those of more fluent students.

I once worked with the theme of travelers with a group of primary and junior students, and we put together a "poetry café," where they read aloud their poems in small groups with great success. Among the poems used were "The Highwayman" by Alfred Noyes and "The Listeners" by Walter de la Mare. The students performed their poems chorally in the cafeteria in front of their parents. They

---

The Conceptual Space around an Image
"In *The Arrival*, the absence of any written description also plants the reader more firmly in the shoes of an immigrant character. There is no guidance as to how the images might be interpreted, and we must ourselves search for meaning and seek familiarity in a world where such things are either scarce or concealed. Words have a remarkable magnetic pull on our attention, and how we interpret attendant images: in their absence, an image can often have more conceptual space around it, and invite a more lingering attention from a reader who might otherwise reach for the nearest convenient caption, and let that rule their imagination."
— Shaun Tan, author of *The Arrival*

As a history-based poem, sean o'huigin's beautiful "ghost horse of the mounties" works well for choral reading, especially for any students studying the Riel Rebellion.

Example: Poetry on the theme of travelers performed at a poetry café

displayed the posters they had made of both imaginary and real desired destinations, and they used various kinds of packed suitcases and bags as props.

7. Collaborative Writing

This strategy allows students to talk themselves into understanding as they work together to make a summary paragraph more precise. Students work with a partner or in a small group to write a paragraph that sums up what they have learned. They might use a sentence starter as a prompt, perhaps "The strangest part is . . . ," "There does not appear to be . . . ," or "What we found most surprising about . . ." Once the students have written their paragraphs, they share their creations with another group or with the class.

Sentence stems or prompts are key to supporting scaffolded talk in classrooms. They scaffold student talk by providing a bridge to conversational structures in academic settings that can become familiar and internalized with the students' oral language development. Sentence stems or prompts are modeled by teachers, and students have multiple opportunities to practice the stems in purposeful conversations. This strategy can be useful in teaching students how to enter a conversation, how to offer suggestions in a conversation, and how to respectfully disagree.

The following sentence stems can be co-constructed with students and then posted as a visual or reference chart in the classroom to give students support during conversations. These sentence stems can be adjusted and used by students in all content areas:

- I think the author's message is . . . because . . .
- Something that I noticed was . . .
- I would add that . . .
- To add to your points, I think that . . .
- I'd like to share a different point of view. My point of view is . . .
- I'm not sure about that. Here is what I'm thinking . . .
- Referring to your idea about . . ., I think . . .

8. Corridor of Voices

Students examine from various perspectives a difficult decision a character faces. The class forms two lines, with students facing one another about two metres apart. They thereby create a corridor wide enough for a person to walk through. A student volunteer takes on the role of the character with a major decision to make and walks down the corridor slowly. As the character walks, students on either side of the corridor voice the conflicting thoughts, feelings, memories, and regrets in the character's mind. Students may use lines from the text, if appropriate. The student in role is then interviewed to find out what decision the character will make based on the voices heard.

Example: The mother in *The Crazy Man* by Pamela Porter

Working with the book *The Crazy Man* and a Grade 6 class, I asked for a volunteer to play the role of the mother before she made the decision to hire Angus, the man from the asylum, to help with the seeding of her fields. The mother had a complicated life. Her husband had just left her, she had a critically ill child, and members of the community were unsupportive because of their bias against the mentally ill — she needed to make a decision.

I asked the class to stand in two lines and to imagine what the mother might be thinking as she made her decision. The volunteer mother walked down the path, listening to the voices in her head come alive. I told the mother to stop at the end of the line and tell us her decision. I then invited the class to interview her to find out how their words had affected what she decided to do: to hire the man from the asylum.

9. Flashbacks

Students explore the relationship between the present and the past by creating short flashback scenes. In a flashback, a character might confront his or her past self or past relationship, thereby allowing students to explore motivations and illuminate the character's present circumstances.

I often work with graphic novels and help students understand how flashbacks are used graphically. The artists juxtapose images, overlapping events that have some relationship to one another although they might have happened hours, days, months, or years apart. I help students see how writers flash-back to the past in the character's memory or even how they can flash-forward, wondering what might happen in the future.

Example: "A Soldier's Grave"

I asked students in Grade 4 to work in small groups of five with a script featuring a woman, a man, and three sergeants as characters. Once they decided who was going to play what role, I asked them to stage the scene, giving thought to how they would transition back and forth from the flashback to the present.

Woman: I have come to find my son's grave.
Man: There are many who died and were buried here.
Woman: Can you help me?
Man: On what date was he killed?
Woman: (***flashback***) Oh! I remember the day that I received news of his death as if it was yesterday. Three sergeants knocked at my door.
Sergeant: Are you Mrs. Brian Snow?
Woman: Yes.
Sergeant: May we come in?
Woman: It is about Richard, isn't it?
Woman: (***the present***) He was killed on June 8, 1944. His name was Richard Snow.
Man: Let me help you find his grave.

Directions to the students:
1. Read through the above script. With a partner, find ways of flashing back to the moment of the young man's death — how can you incorporate that into the script?
2. Next, flash-forward to an event that might have occurred if the soldier had not been killed (e.g., his wedding day or the birth of his first child).
3. Rewrite the entire script incorporating these techniques.

10. Stand by Your Choice

Students act on this strategy in the context of a Gallery Walk (see Chapter 4, pages 101 and 102). They walk around the room alone, examining several displays, pictures, quotations, and/or artifacts that are displayed on the classroom walls. They then find the picture, artifact, quotation, or display that interests them, disturbs them, inspires them, or connects with them the most. The particular focus or purpose of the Gallery Walk is clarified ahead of time. Students stand by their choice and discuss it with the others standing with them who made the same choice. They then report back on the key points about their small-group discussion to the class.

11. Have You Heard...?

Students create gossip connected to one of the characters they are studying in either literature or in history. The gossip might be true or partly true. Working in groups of four or five, they each write a piece of gossip on a slip of paper and put it in the center of the group circle. One by one, they read their pieces of gossip. The group then decides on an order for reading so that the gossip escalates. They can rehearse the Gossip Circle and present it to the class. Each Gossip Circle begins with the line, "Have you heard...?" The groups that are listening to the Gossip Circles ask questions to find out whether there is any truth to the rumors heard.

This strategy is an energizer, and it allows students to create a whole new world connected to the characters. It also encourages them to critically ascertain what could be true and false.

Example: Ophelia's behavior in *Hamlet*

Once, when working with a Grade 12 class studying *Hamlet*, I set up the activity in this way:

> The whole castle is abuzz about what's happened to Ophelia. Rumors of her odd behavior are circulating above and below stairs — among the servants, the courtiers, and even in the higher ranks of the military. Here's a sample:
>
> ***Have you heard...*** *that Ophelia kept one of Hamlet's letters and has ripped it into a hundred pieces — each piece to symbolize the number of days since their romance ended? I heard this from the woman who works in the bedchambers changing the sheets. She says that Ophelia rips the letter every day so that there is always one more piece. She keeps the pieces of the ripped letter out in the open on her dressing table so that everyone can see them. Sometimes, she sprinkles rosewater over the pieces and sings a very sad and slow song. She is truly mad.*
>
> *Signed: John Stead, butler*
>
> **Your turn!** Now try your own hand at writing a piece of gossip about Ophelia. You must identify who you are (by signing your note) and where you heard it.
>
> ***Have you heard...?***

12. Hot Seating

A student volunteers to be put on the "hot seat" in front of the class or a large group. The student takes on the role of a character facing a personal dilemma or critical decision and responds to questions about the character's motives, relationships, decisions, thoughts, opinions, and feelings. This strategy helps everyone (both interviewers and hot-seaters) think out loud about the character and discover new insights. One option is to hot-seat small groups (playing various characters) in front of the whole class. Another option is to hot-seat a character's personal artifacts (see the example below). Students can also play historical characters, famous scientists, or politicians.

The purpose of hot seating is to open up the curriculum for reflection and debate. Students improvise answers to questions, and both hot-seaters and questioners wonder aloud about characters, relationships, incidents, facts, feelings, actions, and consequences. Inventive questions and answers are fodder for debate and discussion.

Example: The desk of Shylock, *The Merchant of Venice*

In a workshop I co-conducted with Belarie Zatzman at the Stratford Festival of Canada, the actors from the Company created Shylock's desk, incorporating newspaper and found objects, and considering what might have been in the drawers, on top, underneath, and so on. The actors also created letters, pages from a diary, and a picture that Shylock's daughter Jessica had drawn of him when she was five years old. I then had each of the actors stand, holding one of these objects, and speak in role as that object. I, of course, was working with the premier actors in Canada, and their improvisational capacities were extraordinary — it was a magical moment in my teaching career.

13. Improvising in Pairs

This strategy helps students understand a character's motivations and recognize tension, conflict, character intentionality, and multiple interpretations. Students work with a partner to improvise a scene. They consider the situation in which the characters find themselves and "break the scene down" so that they discover what each character wants to accomplish in the scene. For example, as part of a study of *Hamlet*, a psychiatrist might want to find out what is going on in Hamlet's life to determine whether he is mad. The other character, playing Hamlet, reacts and makes it as hard as possible for the first character to achieve his goal (Hamlet can be deliberately misleading). The improvisation can be shaped into a prepared scene and shared with another group or with the class.

14. Inner/Outer Circle

Students write in role from at least two different perspectives, for example, parent and child, guidance counselor and student. Those who have written from one perspective sit in a circle with their writing-in-role in hand. The others stand behind with their writing in hand. When the teacher taps the students on the shoulder, they begin reading their writing. As soon as another person is tapped, that student begins to read and the other stops. The teacher goes around the circle, having students read their writing, and orchestrates a mingling of voices and ideas. The same student can read more than once. Students can be given the choice of starting from the beginning or continuing from where they left off. In this way, the class creates a personalized "reading" of a character's predicament, a strained relationship, or a decision that was difficult to make. Multiple perspectives and opposing views are heard.

Example: Jackie Robinson's decision

I worked with a Grade 5 class on the picture book *Teammates* by Peter Golenbock, a story of how Jackie Robinson became the first Black player on a Major League baseball team when he joined the Brooklyn Dodgers in the 1940s. I had the students create five groups of about five members. I assigned each group a role, as listed on the next page:

1. Jackie Robinson's family
2. The members of Jackie Robinson's church
3. Jackie Robinson's school friends
4. The members of the Negro League, where Robinson had played, including the coach
5. Jackie Robinson's teachers

I asked for a volunteer from each group to play the baseball player. I pulled all the Jackie Robinsons aside and asked them to work together to figure out why the Black athlete would make such a big life decision, given the racism and upheaval he would be facing. While the Jackie Robinsons were working on that assignment, I asked the small group members to decide on the kind of advice they would give to the young man. Would they try to dissuade him from making this big decision? What questions would they ask him? On a signal from me, the students playing Jackie Robinson each entered their assigned group, and group members improvised a scene where Robinson meets his friends, family, church members, or members of another group to tell them about his decision. The improvisation lasted for about five minutes.

I then handed out a lined index card to each person and asked the students to write in role about the encounter they had just been a part of.

Once the students had completed their writing, I asked all the Jackie Robinsons to sit on chairs in the middle of the classroom and the other students to form a circle around them. I then staggered the reading out loud of the writing, having the various people in Robinson's life pass on their worries, fears, and advice. I countered those worries with the Robinson voice(s) sharing determination and courage to make a big change that would have an impact on the lives of many to come after the ball player.

15. Interviewing for Insights

In small groups, characters are interviewed by reporters or interrogated by others who question their motives, values, and beliefs, and who want to elicit information. The teacher then asks the interviewers to share new information they have gleaned with the class. Similar to hot seating, this strategy allows students to discover new insights into characters and the texts in which they appear.

I tend to use this strategy a lot when I am working with transactional texts or non-fiction. In one instance, I worked with a Grade 7 class on a piece of text relating to body piercing. I began by asking the students what they knew about it and how safe it was, whether they had any experience with it, and how their parents or guardians felt about it. We then read a piece called "Is Body Piercing Safe?"

Next, I asked the students to get into groups of five. I asked for a volunteer to become a body piercing expert who was looking for a job in a legitimate body piercing parlor. The other students worked with the text to design interview questions. The volunteers worked together to prepare for their interviews. On a signal, the interviews began, and the students remained in role until I asked everyone to stop. I then interviewed members of the hiring committee to see if they would be willing to hire the applicant. I also interviewed some of the applicants to find out which questions they had considered challenging and how they felt they did in answering them.

Taking a Stand

Students could be prompted to decide where they "stand" in relation to a decision a character has made. Either an imaginary line is painted on the floor of the classroom or a rope is laid out, and students stand near, far from, or on the line to make their thoughts and opinions transparent.

After having students do the Inner/Outer Circle strategy on Jackie Robinson, I asked one member of each group to stand close to the line if they thought that Robinson was making a good decision to join the Brooklyn Dodgers and further away if they did not. The representatives then told the rest of the class why they felt the way they did.

Example: Body piercing experts

16. Masks and Movement

Masks can open up new discussions about what texts mean. Beyond that, students who excel in kinesthetic learning have opportunities to demonstrate their understanding of a play in new, imaginative, and innovative ways. They can use their bodies as instruments of communication and meaning making.

Students may create half masks and wear them as they work with short script excerpts to explore the meaning behind the words through movement.

Traditionally, half masks allow actors to speak, but full-faced masks, even with mouth openings, prohibit actors from speaking. So, actors wearing full masks will focus on communicating only with their bodies, finding a way to interpret the scene through movement and gesture.

Often, students find that masks enhance tension between characters, redefine relationships, and create new understandings of the text. Because the use of gesture is amplified by mask wearers, the audience is also affected in new ways.

Example: *The Night of the Gargoyles* by Eve Bunting

Over the years, I have worked with the picture book *The Night of the Gargoyles* in various elementary classrooms. In one instance, a visiting visual artist helped the students design and create gargoyle masks; then, using the text, the students created a coming-alive-at-midnight movement sequence in small groups. They chose the music, created gestures, and worked with me to create strong choreography that brought the text alive in extraordinary ways.

17. Minimal Scripts

Minimal scripts are short conversations that students create between two or three people using lines from the text. Students imagine the place and circumstances that have brought these people together. They choose lines that simplify the scene and break it down to its barest bones. When students say the lines, the essence of the scene is captured in a simple, straightforward way.

Once they have determined the lines, students decide who will read each role. After they have read the script out loud, they discuss with their partner(s) where the characters might be saying these lines and why they are having this conversation. They then read the minimal script, experimenting with as many different locations, motivations, and situations as they can. They can also say their lines in any of the following diverse ways:

> very slowly
> very quickly
> melodramatically
> angrily
> in whispers
> loudly
> pausing after each line
> switching roles
> moving on one line and sitting on the other
> speaking from different corners of the room and moving towards one another
> singing the lines
> eating and chewing an apple in between lines
> with one character following closely behind the other
> with one character speaking all of his/her lines and the other nothing

as if someone is eavesdropping
as if both characters are extremely shy
with one character acting shyly and the other acting aggressively

You might invite students to experiment with some of these presentation options: doing the scene without speech, pausing for a long time between lines, reading the script very fast, and reading the script in whispers.

You could also prompt the student pairs to consider these questions:
- What are all of the things that happen before the first word is spoken?
- What are all of the things that happen after the last word is spoken?
- Who holds all the power in the scene?
- How can the words be said differently so that the power shifts?
- How can the lines be extended so that more is said?

This exercise allows students to "play with the play" and to find the most authentic way to read the script. When students feel that they have got the meaning just right, they read their script out loud to another partner group. They hear suggestions for making it better. For example: Perhaps they need to pause more between lines, or perhaps they would benefit from some props to make the scene more believable. Pairs continue rehearsing, incorporating the ideas of their critics.

Below is a simple minimal script student pairs could explore.

A: I should'a gone to visit Grandma and Grandpa during the holidays.
B: Yeah — you should have.
A: It's a big regret I have.
B: Yeah.
A: I dunno why I didn't. Just somethin' in me, I guess.
B: Yeah, I know.
A: I dunno. They're just so hard on me. They are so uptight about everything. Especially about . . . well, you know.
B: Yeah.
A: Anyway, it's too late now.
B: Yeah. I guess.

18. Quotes Kept Close

As students read various texts about what they are learning and work with others in the classroom, I encourage them to keep track of the words they love — the images that resonate with them, and the quotations they would like to remember, perhaps even memorize. I tell them that they might need these quotations for future reference, for an assignment, or to receive comfort and gain a sense of the power of language. I tell them, "These words are now yours — and you will never regret having them close."

19. Overheard Conversations

Students improvise a scene between two characters. On a signal from the teacher, the students freeze. When the teacher walks by each partner group, the group comes alive for a few minutes so that the class can overhear the conversation between the characters.

For the minimal script provided, you could ask the students what they think happened to tarnish the relationship with the grandparents. Direct them to find a way to tell that story either as a monologue or as a flashback, and then insert that new material into the original script. Have the students, still in pairs, create a 10-line scene between the grandpa and grandma where they talk about these characters in some way.

Lines of Poetry to Ponder

". . . never send to know for whom the bells tolls;
it tolls for thee."
— John Donne, "No Man Is an Island"

"Tell me about your despair, yours, and I will tell you mine."
— Mary Oliver, "Wild Geese"

This strategy allows new information or new tensions to be introduced in a dramatic way without outside interruption. Students simply listen in to the conversations, which are all different, so that they gain an overall taste of what is going on in the room. This theatrical exercise allows students to be witnesses to different stories emanating from improvised work. For example, if studying *Romeo and Juliet*, they might have an opportunity to hear Juliet's mother questioning the nurse: "What information have you been keeping from me and my husband? I want to know where Juliet has been..."

20. Critical Questioning

Students engage in critical inquiry by asking questions of themselves, the text, and others.

1. What do we know?
Students discover their own interpretation of the texts and connect the language and the ideas in the texts to their own lives. They look at texts with a partner or in a small group. They work from their place of understanding to list all that they understand about the text.

2. What do we want to know?
Students think independently, deeply, and critically about the texts, subtexts, and their meaning. They ask critical questions about what they want to know.

3. Who can answer our questions?
Students brainstorm all of the possible people in the text (and beyond) who could answer their questions.

One student in the class plays one of these roles and improvises answers to the questions. Class members are encouraged to ask open-ended questions to which there are multiple answers. In this way students can discuss controversial issues and engage in debate and dialogue. For instance, if studying *Romeo and Juliet*, students could find out more about the type and severity of gang violence in Shakespeare's Verona by asking the Prince questions; or, if studying *Hamlet*, they could interview the ghost of Hamlet's father to find out what his marriage to Queen Gertrude was really like.

21. Readers Theatre

Readers Theatre is a reading strategy that relies on the power of the words in a text and the skill of groups of readers to fully engage an audience in listening to a text. By sharing their work students gain an opportunity to see and hear different interpretations of a single text or to experiment with, listen to, and speak language from a wide range of source material. The goal of each Readers Theatre group is to convey meaning through their interpretive reading of a text.

Students work in groups as readers. The groups can be made up of readers of different abilities. They might work with texts ranging from stories, jokes, and poems to excerpts from a novel or famous speeches. Encourage the students to read the text many times in different ways, experimenting with different roles and combinations of voices. Often, reluctant readers are drawn into the work as they are needed to speak in unison with others, make sound effects with their voices, repeat words or phrases, or read the part of a solo character. Students do not have to memorize their parts; instead, they should be seen to be reading and all readers have to follow the text, know their cues and parts, and rehearse the piece many times with the group so that their performance is fluid. Readers gain

See the description of a Readers Theatre event on pages 45 to 47 in Chapter 2.

confidence as they experiment with ideas, explore the script in different ways, and adjust roles so that everyone feels comfortable. This kind of presentation need not involve costumes, set, or movement. The readers generally stand while reading, using their voices to bring the action of the scene to life in the imaginations of their audience.

22. Role on the Wall

This strategy allows students to juxtapose ideas and concepts, and create a visual "snapshot" of a character to examine. A student volunteers to draw an abstract figure on the chalkboard or interactive whiteboard. The figure should be large enough so that students can write descriptive words and phrases on the inside. These words and phrases may describe that character's psychological, emotional, and physical characteristics. In the space surrounding the figure, students write words that describe the difficulties the character is encountering. Around the figure, students write the names of people or things that are supporting the character. Students are interviewed about why they chose the words they did. Multiple figures can be created so that students can compare characters.

Example: Macbeth and Lady Macbeth

On the chalkboard or on the Smart Board, show outlines of two large-scale figures representing Macbeth and Lady Macbeth. Invite the students to come up and within each figure write descriptive words that apply to the character. This exercise is done in complete silence. Even if someone disagrees with the adjectives being used, nothing is to be said until after everyone has taken part. You could play music as the students fill up the figures with words.

When the words have been exhausted, prompt students to defend their word choices, making references to the text. Ask: "Are there synonyms that can be added? How are these characters different? Why do you think that they are attracted to one another? Who appears to be more powerful? Who is more evil and why?"

23. Soundscapes

Body percussion encompasses hand clapping, toe tapping, foot thumping, chest thumping, stomping, thigh slapping, stepping, finger snapping, and hand warming.

Students work in small groups imagining the essence of a particular setting in the material under discussion (e.g., the rampart, the battlefield, the tomb, the marketplace). They then begin to experiment with different ways to create that environment through sounds — using voice, body percussion, found objects, or simple instruments. They improvise and experiment with volume, pace, tone, tempo, repetition, emotion, and timing to find the most effective combination of sounds that will represent the environment. Students (or the teacher) orchestrate the soundscape as other students listen. The soundscape can be used as a backdrop for scene work by another group.

See the description of a soundscape on pages 93 and 94 in Chapter 4.

24. Storyboarding

Students create a storyboard before they shoot a short film based on a scene in the play or an incident in the historical event they are studying. This activity allows them to imagine what the filming process will be like before they even pick up a camera. They pare down the script, decide on a series of moments, and then create pictures (either drawn or photographed) and texts to represent them. These pictures are similar to cartoon stills that can be brought to life.

Students work in small groups, using one index card for the creation of each shot, or picture. They lay out their cards in order to develop a storyboard that will visually tell the story of their film.

Students decide on the following:
- Which characters are in the frame? What are they doing and how are they moving?
- What are the characters saying to each other?
- What are they doing when not speaking?
- Where is the "camera" in the scene? Close or far away?

Have students draw their storyboard in pen or pencil. If they are worried about drawing, allow them to use still photographs, cutouts from magazines, or computer images. Because they are drawing their storyboard frames on index cards, they will be able to move parts of the story around.

Once the group has agreed on the storyboard, they can film the scene.

25. Tableaux

See pages 91 and 92 for an illustration of tableau use.

Groups of students use their bodies to create frozen pictures that crystallize a key moment, idea, or theme. This strategy requires students to discuss, collaborate, and decide on the image they want to communicate or represent. Tableaux are usually shared in complete stillness and silence. Narration or a reading of text is sometimes added.

Students can experiment with
- different levels (high, medium, low) so that the image is varied in form
- various body shapes (open, closed) to make sure that the important elements in the tableau can be seen by the rest of the class when it is shared
- physical distance between the characters in the tableau as a reflection of their relationship
- what the audience will focus on when the tableau is analyzed
- different kinds of emotions, body language, and facial expression

Movement transitions are often used to connect a series of tableaux. Students walk into their space in a neutral position and then freeze into the tableau.

26. Through the Peephole

A character spies through a peephole to listen in on a conversation between two main characters in a scene. Because the sight lines are limited and it is hard to hear, the peeping character gets a distorted idea of what is going on. In small groups, students create a through-the-peephole scene — cutting lines, sometimes hearing only one character, sometimes not being able to hear at all, and seeing only some of the characters' movements. Often, the characters go out of focus. The conversation is reduced to about 12 lines that ultimately misrepresent what is happening in the scene. Students develop these scenes and then share them with the class. Together, they discuss the various perspectives and potential consequences: the peephole's limitations mean that students have to imagine what they cannot completely see.

Have the students present their through-the-peephole scenes to each other.

Example: Sample directions for through-the-peephole *Hamlet*

Imagine that you are a servant who worked under the old king in a prominent position, but now you find yourself serving under the new king, Claudius, whom you consider a fool. You know that things are not the same, and you feel very hard done by. You decide to listen in on the conversations happening in Gertrude's sewing room but just like the cracked mirror distorts the images in the film, being only able to see from a very small vantage point also distorts your idea of what is going on. It is also hard to hear — and you miss lines and whole passages.

Create the through-the-peephole scene — cutting lines, being able to hear only one character, not being able to hear at all, and being able to only see the characters moving about the room. Often, they go out of focus. At some point you quit because you imagine that someone is in the hallway and will see you . . .

27. Walk-Around Reading

See page 79 for a specific example of the use of Walk-Around Reading.

Students read an assigned text as they walk about the room and listen to other people reading as they walk (the teacher can stagger the readings by touching students on the shoulder). On an agreed-upon signal, everyone stops reading and stands quietly. Students are asked to find their favorite line, phrase, or word (or the line, phrase, or word they consider most powerful or most effective, for example). When touched on the shoulder, they say their line, phrase, or word out loud. In this way students create a new poetry reading, hearing their lines said out loud by different voices in different ways. Students can also share the reasons for their choices, new understandings, and responses with the rest of the class.

As part of an equity-focused workshop with Junior students in a school in Mississauga, I worked with the text of Malala Yousafzai's speech given at the United Nations on 12 July 2013. The inspiring speech appears within the book of photos entitled *Every Day Is Malala Day*, by Rosemary McCarney with Plan International. The students were given the full text of the speech and found their individual favorite lines, words, or phrases. I watched as the English Language Learners listened to others walking around the room. They checked for pronunciation and quietly practiced their line out loud without pressure.

Example: Speech at the United Nations by Nobel Prize–winning Malala Yousafzai

I began by listening to all the favorite lines, words, or phrases and then I staggered the reading so that the outcome was beautiful and intense. I played music in the background.

Here is some of the text from the transcript:

One child
I speak not for myself
Myself
One teacher
The left side of my forehead
Poverty, injustice and ignorance
Education first
One child
I speak not for myself
Myself

Developing a Scene

An extension of Walk-Around Reading is to have students find a partner and share their word or line. They then develop a scene where only those words or lines are said in a dramatic context out loud. The only rule: The lines can be repeated, but no new lines or words can be added.

Strength power and courage
No one
No one can stop us
One pen
The power and strength of words
One book
Unity and togetherness
Bright and peaceful future
Our most powerful weapons
The weapon of knowledge

One child
I speak not for myself
Myself
The weapon of knowledge

28. Teacher in Role

I have used this technique hundreds of times in classrooms as I introduce themes, novels, and historical events. What appeals to students and surprises them is that the teacher is willing to shift the classroom dynamic — to give over power to them for a period of time. The role-playing unlocks new avenues of understanding and allows students to relate to the characters they are meeting with an immediacy both enjoyable and memorable. It also lets them practice different language registers as they speak as adults with some authority or experience.

I usually begin this way: "When I turn around, I am going to pretend to be someone other than who I am. I will carefully introduce myself and give you clues as to what my role is. I also will be letting you know in subtle ways who you are. Listen carefully for the clues that I am going to give to you. You do not have to say anything, but let your minds and imaginations be open to the possibilities of this dramatic encounter. When I turn back around, I will be myself again, and we will talk as ourselves about who we were, where we were, what was going on in the story, and what can happen next."

When you as teacher decide to assume a role, be careful to prepare for it and keep in mind that you have to give a clear definition of who you are, where you are, and what is happening so that the class begins to understand the context. Take your time and do not give away more information than is necessary. In this way you can introduce nuance and subtlety and help students understand that an author spends much time leading readers into a story — leading them on so that they will want to read more.

Example: Working with *Journey to Jo'burg* by Beverly Naidoo

Sometimes, I go in role as a character from a book and involve the class that way. I have used the following excerpt and asked the class to become members of a medical team in a clinic. They took on the roles of doctors, nurses, and technicians in small groups. As 13-year-old Naledi, I then entered each of these groups and asked for their help. This is what I said to begin:

> My baby sister, Dineo, has been very, very ill for three days now. My granny has been trying to cool her fever with damp cloths placed on her little head and body. My aunt makes her take little sips of water but she spits them up. We've brought her here for you to help make her well. Can you?

29. The Wave

This movement exercise is a shared experience that relies upon a group's ability to bond with one another and communicate nonverbally. Students walk in unison, shoulder to shoulder, and spontaneously drop out of the line to create statues or shapes that reflect the themes, issues, emotions, ideas, or characters being explored.

Instructions

1. Divide the class into groups of about seven to nine people. While one group works, the other groups stand on both sides of the room to watch.
2. The working group stands at one end of the room, shoulder to shoulder in a straight line, almost touching elbows.
3. The group is to begin moving simultaneously forward, cross the room, turn around and return, all while maintaining their close, straight-line formation. Let each group repeat the crossing at least a couple of times before stopping them.
4. When all groups have practiced, add music to the work, if desired.
5. The next step is to create statues. As the group crosses the room, anyone in line may "fall out" and create a statue or shape that represents the character's feelings, thoughts, or reactions. The rest of the students keep walking.
6. Statues stay frozen until the Wave returns. Statues may wait for more than one passing of the Wave to be enveloped. By so doing, they give the onlookers more time to look at how they are positioned.
7. While the working group performs, the audience's task is to observe and reflect upon the experience.

The Wave as Journey
I have used the Wave to depict journeys, both real and symbolic. Students have created the journey that Lucia from *The Woman Who Outshone the Sun* took after she was driven from the village. A Grade 12 English class once represented Lady Macbeth's journey into madness. The onlooker students stood at the side and watched the various statue interpretations of Lady Macbeth. I then asked the onlookers to represent the horrified, suspicious courtiers in tableau formations on either side of the classroom. A student portrayed Macbeth himself as a terrified onlooker.

30. Writing in Role

Students write from the perspective of a character whom they have explored in a role-playing situation. For example, the students who responded to Jackie Robinson's decision to play Major League baseball (see strategy #14) were able to write with some authority as Robinson or of one of the people around him. Often, students who write in role discover a different and more secure voice because they are writing from "inside the experience." Writing in role allows students' imaginations to play on what they have perceived.

Students can also write in the character of artifacts. See pages 89 to 91 in Chapter 4.

Never Looking Back

I have been fortunate to have taught in exciting, turbulent, politicized, and changing times in education. Whatever has been going on outside the classroom has been of interest to me. I am aware of the pressures to adapt to new ideas and adopt new strategies. I make sure I understand why I am being asked to work in this way, and I try my best to incorporate new technologies into my teaching and be accountable on every level. However, no matter what I am hearing and reading about, no matter what I am being asked to do or learn, I have remained true to what I believe about teaching and learning: that classrooms are negotiated spaces where relationships, power, and identity have as much sway as energy, intellectual capacity, and commitment.

Belief in classrooms as negotiated spaces

I believe that teachers need to be fascinated by who is in their classrooms, to be open to trying new things, to work towards empathetic response, to risk adventure in the interaction between themselves and their students, and to be critical of what is working and what is not. I also believe that teachers need to be willing to connect who they are, where they are from, and what they want to achieve to what they know about their subject, about the curriculum, about the locations and identities of their students, and about the ever-changing world and how it works.

Belief in respect, rich learning, and student potential

I know that respectful relationships matter — not only personal relationships between teachers, students, colleagues, the community, and parents/guardians but also the relationship and respect we should have to the work: to the curriculum that lies before us.

I believe that there are ways to weave a tapestry of teaching together, incorporating various threads of many colors, widths, and textures so that the learning is intellectual, emotional, and transformational all at the same time.

Ultimately, I believe that teachers' pedagogical signatures can flourish as long as they believe that classrooms are places of possibility where all students have a chance at the prize — to be successful — so that eventually they can lead happy and useful lives.

I hope that this book has provided teachers with ideas and inspiration so that they will move forward, try new things, learn about themselves and their students in innovative ways, and never look back.

Bibliography

Andrei, Mihai. 2015. "A Revolution in Education: Finland to Stop Teaching Individual Topics." *ZME Science* (March 25).

Ayers, William. 1988. "'The Long Trip': An Exploration of Progressive Public Schools." *Teaching Education* 2 (2): 88–93.

Ayers, William. 2001. *To Teach: The Journey of a Teacher*, 2nd ed. New York: Teachers College Press.

Ayers, William. 2004. *Teaching the Personal and the Political: Essays on Hope and Justice.* New York: Teachers College Press.

Ayers, William. 2004. "The New School." *Rethinking Schools* (Fall). http://www.rethinkingschools.org/publication/newteacher/ntbegin.shtml.

Baldwin, Patrice, and Kate Fleming. 2003. *Teaching Literacy through Drama: Creative Approaches.* New York: RoutledgeFalmer.

Barth, Roland S. 1990. *Improving Schools from Within: Teachers, Parents and Principals Can Make the Difference.* San Francisco, CA: Jossey-Bass.

Barth, Roland S. 2006. "Improving Relationships within the Schoolhouse." *Improving Professional Practice* 63 (6): 8–13.

Bateson, Mary Catherine. 1990. *Composing a Life: The Age of Active Wisdom.* New York: Grove Press.

Bishop, Peter C., and Andy Hines. 2012. *Teaching about the Future.* New York: Palgrave Macmillan.

Booth, David. 2013. *I've Got Something to Say: How Student Voices Inform Our Teaching.* Markham, ON: Pembroke.

Caine, Geoffrey, and Renate Caine. 1991. *Making Connections: Teaching and the Human Brain.* Wheaton, MD: Association for Supervision and Curriculum Development.

Christensen, Linda. 2000. *Reading, Writing, Rising Up: Teaching about Social Justice and the Power of the Written Word.* Milwaukee, WI: Rethinking Schools.

Clemens, Sydney Gurewitz. *Art in the Classroom* (blog), http://webshares.northseattle.edu/fam180/topics/art/Art%20in%20the%20Classroom.htm.

Delpit, Lisa, ed. 1996. *Other People's Children: Cultural Conflict in the Classroom.* New York: New Press.

Egan, Kieran. 1999. *Children's Minds, Talking Rabbits, and Clockwork Oranges: Essays on Education.* New York: Teachers College Press.

Eisner, Elliot. 1997. *Christian Science Monitor* (January 30).

Freire, Paulo. 1985. "Reading the World and Reading the Word: An Interview with Paulo Freire." *Language Arts* 62 (1): 15–21.

Ginott, Haim. 1972. *Teacher and Child: A Book for Parents and Teachers.* New York: Macmillan.

Green, Joan, Kathleen Gould Lundy, and Jennifer Glass. 2011. *Talking to Learn.* Toronto: Oxford University Press.

Greenberg, Herbert M. 1969. *Teaching with Feeling: Compassion and Self-Awareness in the Classroom Today.* New York: Macmillan.

Greene, Maxine. 2001. *Variations on a Blue Guitar: Uncoupling from the Ordinary.* New York: Teachers College Press.

Grumet, Madeleine R. 1991. "Curriculum and the Art of Daily Life." In *Reflections from the Heart of Educational Inquiry: Understanding Curriculum and Teaching through the Arts,* edited by George Willis and William H. Schubert. New York: State University of New York Press.

James, Carl E. 2004. "Urban Education: An Approach to Community-Based Education." *Intercultural Education* 15 (1): 15–32.

Johnson, David W., and Frank P. Johnson. 2014. *Joining Together: Group Theory and Group Skills,* 11th ed. Harlow, UK: Pearson Education.

Ladson-Billings, Gloria. 1995. "But That's Just Good Teaching! The Case for Culturally Relevant Pedagogy." *Theory into Practice* 34 (3): 159–65.

McIntosh, Peggy. 1988. "White Privilege and Male Privilege: A Personal Account of Coming to See Correspondences through Work in Women's Studies." Wellesley, MA: Wellesley College, Center for Research on Women.

Miller, John P. 1988. *The Holistic Curriculum.* Toronto: OISE Press.

Milton, Penny. 2015. *Shifting Minds 3.0: Redefining the Learning Landscape in Canada.* C21 Canada.

Ontario Ministry of Education. 2009. *Realizing the Promise of Diversity: Ontario's Equity and Inclusive Education Strategy.* www.edu.gov.on.ca.

Schmidt-Jones, Catherine. n.d. "Notes on Questions." https://legacy.cnx.org/content/m45070/latest/.

Soloman, R. Patrick, and Cynthia Levine-Rasky. 1996. "When Principle Meets Practice: Teachers' Contradictory Response to Antiracist Education." *Alberta Journal of Educational Research* 42 (1): 19–33.

Suzuki, David. 1997. *The Sacred Balance: Rediscovering Our Place in Nature.* Vancouver: Douglas and McIntyre.

Torbe, Mike, and Peter Medway. 1981. *Language, Teaching and Learning: A Climate for Learning.* East Grinstead, UK: Ward Lock Educational.

Vars, Gordon F., and James A. Beane. 2000. *Integrative Curriculum in a Standards-Based World.* Champaign, IL: ERIC Clearinghouse on Elementary and Early Childhood Education.

Willms, J. Douglas, Sharon Friesen, and Penny Milton. 2009. *What Did You Do in School Today? Transforming Classrooms through Social, Academic, and Intellectual Engagement* (First National Report). Toronto: Canadian Education Association.

Wolk, Ron. 2010. "Education: The Case for Making It Personal." *Reimagining School* 67 (7): 16–21.

Index

academic (institutional) engagement, 50
Acadian Expulsion, 83–88
achieving insight, 26–27
active listening, 77–79, 120
ambiguity, 110–11
anthology presentations, 99–100
applause, 19
arresting questions, 50
artifacts
   using in teaching, 89–90
   working with, 90
   writing in role, 85, 90–91
artist trading cards, 120–21
artistry, 112
artists, 97
arts and crafts, 81–83
arts strategies
   active, collective listening and response, 120
   artist trading cards, 120–21
   bird's-eye view, 121
   brainstorming, 121–22
   bursting the bubble, 122–23
   choral speaking, 123–24
   collaborative writing, 124
   corridor of voices, 124–25
   critical questioning, 131
   flashbacks, 125
   Have You Heard . . . ?, 126
   hot seating, 126–27
   improvising in pairs, 127
   Inner/Outer Circle, 127–28
   interviewing for insights, 128
   masks and movement, 129
   minimal scripts, 129–30
   overheard conversations, 130–31
   quotes kept close, 130
   Readers Theatre, 131–32
   role on the wall, 132
   soundscapes, 132
   Stand by Your Choice, 125–26
   storyboarding, 132–33
   tableaux, 133
   teacher in role, 135
   Through the Peephole, 133–34
   Walk-Around Reading, 134–35
   Wave, 136
   writing in role, 136
assessment, 53

bird's-eye view, 121
bodystorming, 86–87
brainstorming, 121–22
bursting the bubble, 122–23

checklist for achievement, 102
choral speaking, 123–24
classrooms as negotiated spaces, 137
CLEAR Criteria rubric, 69
collaborative inquiry, 49, 54–55
collaborative talk, 51
collaborative teaching, 71–73
collaborative writing, 124
collective drama, 97
collegiality, 54
community
   acting as stakeholder in, 27–28
   fostering teachers' sense of, 27–28
   reaching out to, 28
   school, 34–35
community-based education, 10–11
conceptual teaching, 49–50
co-operative games, 17–19
corridor of voices, 124–25
critical listening, 20–22
critical questioning, 131
culminating events, 99–102
cultural lens, 13
culturally responsive and relevant pedagogy, 30
curators (group work), 67
curriculum as tapestry, 7, 8, 72, 95–96, 103
curriculum integration
   described, 71–72
   team approach, 103
curriculum questions, 33

dance, 97
digital talk, 52–53
disappearance theme, 88–96

diversity, 33–34
drama and history, 87–88, 95–96
dynamic teaching, 113–16

education system, 35
effective teaching
    characteristics, 108
    pedagogical signature, 108–12
    reflection questions, 112
    six Es of effective teaching, 112–13
embracing challenges, 24
emotional connections, 122
empathy, 15–17
English Language Learners (ELLs), 36, 61
equality, 24
equity, 24, 30–31, 35
Expert Game, 60

fascination about learning, 108–9
First Nation, Métis, and Inuit (FNMI), 45–47, 81–83
5 Ws, 63–65
Flashbacks, 125
Four Kinds of Questions, 58
freeze frame, 91
From I to We creative activity, 40–45

Gallery Walks, 101–2, 125–26
gossip, 126
group constellations, 65
group processing skills
    appreciation of, 110
    teaching, 65–66
groups
    defining roles and responsibilities, 67
    promoting positive interactions, 66–67
    sharing findings and understandings, 67–68
    teaching processing skills, 65–66, 110

Have You Heard . . .?, 126
history and drama, 87–88, 95–96
hot seating, 58–60, 76, 126–27
How to Support Research, 70

I Am From . . . poetry exercise, 41–42
I Am Now From . . . poetry exercise, 45
I See, I Remember, I Imagine . . ., 77
identity games
    Ball Game with Words and Phrases, 39
    Ball Throw, 38
    My Name Has Meaning, 39
    Name Call Ball Toss, 38–39
    Name Switch Now, 38
    Say Your Name, 38
    The Seat on My Right Is Free, 38
improvisation, 21, 109, 127

inclusion activities/exercises
    Atom, 17
    Back to Back/Face to Face, 18
    Birthday Line, 18
    Do as I Say, 20
    Fortunately/Unfortunately, 21
    "Good Morning, Your Esteemed Majesty," 21
    Heigh Ho!, 19
    Let's Just Listen, 20
    No One Sees . . ., 23
    Reading Identity, 22
    Squirrel and Tree, 19
    Stomp It, Name It, Clap It, 18–19
    Two Truths and a Wish, 21–22
inclusion practices, 24–27
inclusive classrooms, 9–10
inclusive talk, 52
information gatherers (group work), 67
informed talk, 52
Inner/Outer Circle, 127–28
innovation questions, 107
inquiry-based classroom
    described, 48–49
    questions, 55–56
inquiry process
    honoring student voice, 50–53
    improving student achievement, 53
    increasing student engagement, 49–50
    purposes, 49
    refining teacher practice, 54
inquiry project models
    Grey Matter, 97
    Imagine a Place, Imagine a Time, 97
    Into the Woods, 98
    Looking at the Over-Looked, 97
    Lost, But Not Forgotten, 97
    models, 96–98
    Planting the Seeds of Proportional Reasoning, 98
    Seeing with New Eyes, 97
    Shining a Light on School Stigmas, 97
    Stand in the Place Where You Live, 97
    steps to fulfilling, 55
    Time Is Precious, 98
inquiry questions
    criteria, 54
    developing, 57–65
    Expert Game, 60
    5 Ws approach, 63–65
    four kinds, 56
    from question to question, 57–58
    hot seating, 58–60
    students in professional roles asking questions, 62–63
    teacher in role, 61–62
integration
    approaches to, 73–74